Direct Hits Core Vocabulary of the SAT: Volume 1

2011 Edition

By Larry Krieger

Edited by Ted Griffith

This copy belongs to:

_____

For more information, contact us at:

Direct Hits Publishing
2639 Arden Rd., Atlanta GA 30327
Ted@DirectHitsPublishing.com

Visit our website at:
www.DirectHitsPublishing.com

Third Edition: August 2010

ISBN 10:   0-9818184-5-5

ISBN 13:   978-0-9818184-5-0

Edited by Ted Griffith

Cover Design by Carlo da Silva

Interior Design by Katherine Goodman

Acknowledgements

This book would not have been possible without the help of great students, dedicated friends and a tireless Product Manager. I would like to thank the following students for their valuable suggestions: Kate Armstrong, Jacob Byrne, Jill Reid, Lindsey Brenner, Misha Milijanic, Britney Frankel, Charlie Griffith, and Joey Holland. Special thanks to Lauren Treene, Evan Hewel, Holland McTyeire, and Alex Washington for their ability to help me connect vivid movie scenes with difficult SAT words.

I would also like to thank Jan Altman for her original research compiling lists of key SAT words. As always, Jane Armstrong's unfailing enthusiasm inspired our creative energies. Additionally, thank you to Jane Saral for careful proofreading and clarification of all grammar questions. Extra special thanks to Claire Griffith for her encouragement and creative ideas, and to Luther Griffith for his keen insights and impeccable judgment.

This book would not have been possible without a dedicated Product Manager. Ted Griffith has been everything an author could ask for - resourceful, innovative, and meticulous.

And finally, I am deeply grateful for the "close reads," patience, and love of my wife, Susan.

Table of Contents

Introduction

Have you ever visited a country where the people spoke a language you didn't understand? If you have had this experience, you may have vivid memories of misreading signs, ordering wrong foods, and feeling frustrated by not understanding what is going on around you.

Many students complain that taking the PSAT and the SAT is like trying to understand a foreign language. The critical reading and sentence completion quest-ions do contain a number of difficult words. For example, recent SATs included many challenging words such as acquiesce.

Although these words may seem obscure, they are actually everyday words that appear in newspapers, books, and even movies. For example, in *Pirates of the Caribbean: The Curse of the Black Pearl*, Elizabeth Swann and Captain Barbossa conduct negotiations that include the word acquiesce. Although he claims to be a "humble pirate," Captain Barbossa does understand what the "long word" acquiesce means. He firmly rejects Swann's demands, saying, "I'm disinclined to acquiesce to your request. Means no!"

Why is having a rich vocabulary that includes words such as acquiesce important? Words are among our most valuable tools for learning and communicating. As your vocabulary increases, you will become more articulate. As an articulate person, you will be able to speak more eloquently and write more convincingly.

Introduction

Researchers have shown that a superior vocabulary is strongly associated with success in school, business, the professions, and standardized tests such as the PSAT and SAT.

Learning new words doesn't have to be a tedious chore. I believe that augmenting your vocabulary can be fun. I've selected 400 challenging words that have appeared on recent SATs. The first 200 are in this volume and the second 200 words are in Volume 2. Each word is illustrated with vivid examples taken from popular movies, TV shows, and significant historic events and figures tested on AP US History, AP European History, AP World History, and AP Art History exams. This mix of pop culture and history is based upon the old childhood rhyme that "what's learned with pleasure is learned full measure."

I hope you enjoy learning the vocabulary words in Volume 1. I also want you to test your ability to use these words. Each SAT includes 19 sentence completion questions worth 35 percent of your Critical Reading score. You'll find a set of 10 sentence completion questions at the end of each chapter. They will give you an opportunity to test your vocabulary on SAT questions. Answers and a detailed explanation of each question follow each set of questions.

So what are you waiting for? Turn to the first two pages. You'll find Finn Hudson (*Glee*), Vernon Dursley (*Harry Potter and the Sorcerer's Stone*), and Dr. Grace Augustine (*Avatar*) all waiting and eager to help you AUGMENT (increase) your vocabulary.

About Larry Krieger

Larry Krieger is one of the foremost SAT experts in the country. His renowned teaching methods and SAT prep courses are praised for both their inventive, engaging approaches and their results. Students under Krieger's guidance improve their SAT scores by an average of 200 points.

Formerly a social studies supervisor and AP Art History teacher at New Jersey's SAT powerhouse Montgomery Township High School near Princeton, Krieger led the school to a Number 1 ranking in the state and nation for a comprehensive public high school. In 2004, Montgomery students achieved a record national average score of 629 on the Critical Reading section of the SAT.

Beginning in 2005, the College Board recognized Krieger's AP Art History course as the "strongest in the world" for three straight years. With an open enrollment, 60 percent of the senior class took the course and 100 percent made grades of 3 or higher, including some special education students.

Krieger is the co-author of several US History, World History, and AP Art History texts used throughout the country. He earned a BA in history and an MAT from University of North Carolina at Chapel Hill and an MA in sociology from Wake Forest.

Though Krieger admits to being completely unprepared for his first SAT in high school, he regularly takes the SAT to keep up with changes on the new test.

Chapter 1

CORE VOCABULARY I: 1–50

The English language contains just over one million words – the most of any language in human history. If each of these words had an equal chance of being used on the SAT, studying for the test would be a truly impossible task.

Fortunately, the pool of words used by Educational Testing Service (ETS) test writers is actually relatively small. Many key words are repeatedly tested. This is particularly true of Level 3 and 4 words that over half of the test-takers (students like you!) do not know. These words are crucial to achieving a high Critical Reading score.

These crucial mid-level words form the core LEXICON or special vocabulary you need to know to score well on the Critical Reading portion of the SAT. Based upon a careful analysis of recent tests, we have identified 100 Core Vocabulary Words. The first 50 of these words are in Chapter 1 and the second 50 are in Chapter 2. The division is arbitrary. Each word is a high frequency word that you absolutely, positively must know.

1. AMBIVALENT:
Contradictory, having mixed feelings

In the TV show *Glee*, Finn Hudson is the star quarterback of his high school football team. Finn is also a talented singer who is AMBIVALENT about joining the school Glee Club. Although Finn doesn't want to alienate his teammates, he enjoys singing and wants to follow his dream of becoming an entertainer.

In the movie *The Notebook*, Allie has to choose between Noah and Lon. She is emotionally torn by her AMBIVALENT feelings as she tells Noah, "There is no easy way, no matter what I do, somebody gets hurt." She later reiterates her AMBIVALENT feelings when she tells Lon, "When I'm with Noah, I feel like one person, and when I'm with you, I feel like someone totally different."

2. ANOMALY:
Deviation from the norm, something that is ATYPICAL

In the Harry Potter series, Vernon Dursley prides himself on being "perfectly normal, thank you very much." An ANOMALY is the last thing Dursley wants in his life. In the opening chapter of *Harry Potter and the Sorcerer's Stone*, however, Dursley notices several strange ANOMALIES or what he calls "funny stuff." For example, he spots a cat that appears to be reading a map. He also notices a number of odd people who are dressed in colorful robes. And that is not all: flocks of owls can be seen flying during the daytime.

3. SARCASTIC, SARDONIC, SNIDE:
Mocking, derisive, taunting, and stinging

Winston Churchill was famous for his SARCASTIC and SARDONIC comments. Here are two well-known examples:

> *Bessie Braddock*: Sir, you are a drunk.
>
> *Churchill*: Madame, you are ugly. In the morning I shall be sober, and you will still be ugly.
>
> *Nancy Astor*: Sir, if you were my husband I would give you poison.
>
> *Churchill*: If I were your husband I would take it.

In the movie *Avatar*, Dr. Grace Augustine tells Jake, "Just relax and let your mind go blank. That shouldn't be too hard for you." This SNIDE remark expresses Grace's initial contempt for Jake.

4. DEARTH and PAUCITY:
A scarcity or shortage of something

A study by *USA Today* revealed that college football's top level teams have a DEARTH of minority coaches. Just 10 of the 120 Football Bowl Subdivision universities have minority head coaches. There is also a PAUCITY of minority assistant coaches. In contrast, about one-fourth of the 32 NFL teams have minority head coaches. Critics encourage the colleges to EMULATE (imitate) the NFL's policy of requiring teams to interview minority candidates for head coaching opportunities.

5. PRATTLE:
To speak in a foolish manner, to babble incessantly

In the movie *Office Space*, Milton continuously PRATTLES to himself about how he is abused by management and how his co-workers repeatedly borrow his stapler. Here is an example of Milton PRATTLING on and on:

> *"I don't care if they lay me off either, because I told, I told Bill that if they move my desk one more time, then, then, I'm, I'm quitting, I'm going to quit. And, I told Don too, because they've moved my desk four times already this year, and I used to be over by the window, and I could see the squirrels, and they were married, but then, they switched from the Swingline to the Boston stapler, but I kept my Swingline stapler because it didn't bind up as much, and I kept the staplers for the Swingline stapler and it's not okay, because if they take my stapler then I'll set the building on fire ..."*

6. WRY:
Dry, humorous with a clever twist and a touch of irony; DROLL

Casel Di Principe is normally a sleepy town northwest of Naples, Italy. On a quiet Sunday a 60-year-old man sat at a table playing cards with his friends. Two gunmen suddenly shattered the peace when they drove down the town's main street and fired a barrage of bullets, killing the old man. The assassination of an important crime boss caused authorities to launch a full-scale investigation. However, the witnesses refused to answer questions, claiming that they didn't see anything. Their collective silence prompted a WRY comment from one police officer that "the victim must have been playing solitaire."

Tip for a Direct Hit

A WRY sense of humor is very different from a JOCULAR sense of humor. A WRY joke appeals to your intellect and often produces a knowing smile. In contrast, a JOCULAR joke appeals to your funny bone and produces a belly laugh.

7.   **UNCONVENTIONAL and UNORTHODOX:**
      Not ordinary or typical; characterized by avoiding customary conventions and behaviors

Both Katy Perry and Lady Gaga are known for their catchy hits and bold, UNCONVENTIONAL wardrobes. Katy Perry's colorful, UNORTHODOX costumes include a funky playing cards dress, a watermelon dress, and a cute pink panda outfit.

Lady Gaga is also known for wearing UNCONVENTIONAL and even OUTLANDISH (bizarre, outrageous) stage outfits. Gaga is usually attired in her trademark platinum blonde hair, funky sunglasses, and revealing leotards. However, she is always unpredictable. Gaga opened one concert wearing clear plastic champagne bubbles and then changed into a sculpted prom dress.

8. PAINSTAKING and METICULOUS:
Extremely careful; very EXACTING

The new Harry Potter theme park is a METICULOUS recreation of Hogwarts castle and nearby Hogsmeade village. The park's designers spared no expense to PAINSTAKINGLY recreate such iconic rooms as Dumbledore's office and the Defense Against the Dark Arts classroom. ENTHRALLED (fascinated) visitors can sample butterbeer and even purchase a wand at Ollivander's Wand Shop.

audacious

9. AUDACIOUS:
Fearlessly, often recklessly daring; very bold

What do American General George Washington and Japanese Admiral Isoroku Yamamoto have in common? Both launched AUDACIOUS surprise attacks on unsuspecting adversaries. On Christmas Day, 1776, Washington ordered the Colonial Army to cross the Delaware and attack the British and Hessian forces at Trenton. Washington's AUDACIOUS plan shocked the British and restored American morale. On December 7, 1941, Yamamoto ordered the Japanese First Air Fleet to launch a surprise attack on the American Pacific Fleet based at Pearl Harbor. Although Japan's AUDACIOUS sneak attack temporarily HOBBLED (hampered) the U.S. fleet, it aroused the now unified country to demand revenge.

indifferent   *apathetic*

10. INDIFFERENT and APATHETIC:
Marked by a lack of interest or concern

In the movie *Ferris Bueller's Day Off*, the economic teacher Ben Stein delivers a SOPORIFIC (sleep-inducing) lecture on tariffs and the Great Depression. Stein's bored and INDIFFERENT students ignore his monotone lecture. Hoping for some sign of interest, Stein tries asking questions, but his efforts are FUTILE (Word 46). Some students are so APATHETIC they fall asleep.

11. DIFFIDENT:
Lacking self-confidence; self-effacing; NOT assertive

Even Lady Gaga wakes up and feels like an insecure and DIFFIDENT 24-year-old girl. But Gaga then tells herself, "You're Lady Gaga, you get up and walk the walk today." As you study for the SAT, be like Lady Gaga. Don't SUCCUMB (give in) to feelings of DIFFIDENCE. Study your *Direct Hits* vocabulary and be confident.

12. PRAGMATIC:
Practical; sensible; NOT idealistic or romantic

What do the 16th century French king Henry IV and the 20th century American president Franklin Delano Roosevelt have in common? Both leaders made PRAGMATIC decisions that helped resolve a crisis. Henry IV was the newly crowned Protestant king in a country dominated by Catholics. For the sake of his war-weary country, Henry IV PRAGMATICALLY chose to become a Catholic, saying, "Paris is worth a Mass."

FDR was a newly-elected president in a country facing the worst economic crisis in its history. For the sake of his country, Roosevelt PRAGMATICALLY chose to replace traditional laissez-faire economic policies with "bold, persistent experimentation." FDR PRAGMATICALLY explained, "It is common sense to take a method and try it; if it fails, admit it frankly and try another. But above all, try something."

13. EVOCATION:
An imaginative re-creation

What do the treasures of Pharaoh Tutankhamen, Taylor Swift's music video "Love Story," and the movie *Titanic* all have in common? They are all powerful EVOCATIONS. The treasures of Pharaoh Tutankhamen are EVOCATIONS of the power and splendor of Ancient Egypt. Taylor Swift's "Love Story" EVOKES a time when beautiful princesses lived in romantic castles and fell in love with handsome princes. And the movie *Titanic* is a remarkable EVOCATION of what it was like to be a passenger on the great but doomed ship.

14. PRESUMPTUOUS:
Overbearing; impertinently bold; characterized by brashly overstepping one's place

In the movie *300*, Queen Gorgo boldly told the Persian envoy, "Do not be coy or stupid, Persian. You can afford neither in Sparta." Queen Gorgo's willingness to speak out astonished the Persian envoy. Shocked by the Spartan Queen's PRESUMPTUOUS statement, the envoy questioned, "What makes this woman think she can speak among men?"

15. RECALCITRANT:
Stubborn resistance to and defiance of authority or guidance; OBSTINATE; OBDURATE

What do Hester Prynne (*The Scarlet Letter*) and the singer Amy Winehouse have in common? Both are RECALCITRANT. In *The Scarlet Letter*, the Reverend Wilson demanded that Hester reveal the name of the father of her child. But Hester was RECALCITRANT. Despite "the heavy weight of a thousand eyes, all fastened upon her," Hester stubbornly refused to name the father, defiantly declaring, "Never...I will not speak!" In her song "Rehab," Amy Winehouse is also defiantly RECALCITRANT. Her friends and family all beg her to go to rehab, but Amy is OBDURATE and defiantly declares, "No, no, no."

16. BOON:
A timely benefit; blessing

BANE:
A source of harm and ruin

Fifty Cent was shot nine times and lived! Was the shooting a BANE or a BOON for his career? At first it was a BANE because the pain was excruciating and Fiddy had to spend weeks in a hospital recuperating. But the shooting turned out to be a BOON for his career because it BOLSTERED (reinforced) Fiddy's "street cred" and attracted lots of publicity.

17. CLANDESTINE and SURREPTITIOUS:
Secret; covert; not open; NOT ABOVEBOARD

What do the Men in Black (*Men In Black*), Dumbledore's Army (*Harry Potter and the Order of* the *Phoenix*), and Sector Seven (*Transformers*) all have in common? They are all CLANDESTINE groups that conduct SURREPTITIOUS activities. The Men in Black SURREPTITIOUSLY regulate alien life forms on Earth. Dumbledore's Army teaches Hogwarts students how to defend themselves against the Dark Arts. And Sector Seven guards the mysterious All Spark and keeps the body of Megatron permanently frozen.

18. AFFABLE, AMIABLE, GENIAL, GREGARIOUS:
All mean agreeable; marked by a pleasing personality; warm and friendly

President Reagan was renowned for his AFFABLE grace and GENIAL good humor. On March 6, 1981, a deranged gunman shot the president as he was leaving a Washington hotel. The injured but always AMIABLE president looked up at his doctors and nurses and said, "I hope you're all Republicans." The first words he uttered upon regaining consciousness were to a nurse who happened to be holding the president's hand. "Does Nancy know about us?" the president joked.

Tip for a Direct Hit

If you think you have heard the word AMIABLE before, you are probably right. The English word AMIABLE contains the Latin root *ami* meaning friend. You may have heard this root in the French word *ami* and the Spanish word *amigo*.

19. AUSTERE:
Having no adornment or ornamentation; bare; not ORNATE (Word 363)

AUSTERITY:
The trait of great self-denial; economy

Ancient Greek architects often used Doric columns to construct temples. For example, the Parthenon's AUSTERE columns conveyed strength and simplicity because they lacked ornamentation.

Although modern Greeks admire the AUSTERE columns built by their ancestors, they vigorously oppose new AUSTERITY measures that raise taxes and cut social welfare programs. These AUSTERITY measures have provoked massive protests.

20. ALTRUISTIC:
Unselfish concern for the welfare of others

Eleven-year-old Olivia Bouler sobbed uncontrollably when she first saw pictures of oil-coated birds dying along the Gulf coast. Rather than continue to cry, Olivia wrote a letter to the Audubon Society offering to help. Olivia volunteered to draw and sell watercolor paintings of birds and give the profits to the Audubon Society. Olivia's ALTRUISTIC campaign has helped raise over $160,000 to save Gulf birds.

21. AMBIGUOUS:
Unclear; uncertain; open to more than one interpretation; not definitive

The final scene of the movie *Inception* is deliberately AMBIGUOUS. Leo DiCaprio's character, Dom Cobb, is ELATED (very happy) because he has found his children and completed the seemingly impossible job he was hired to do. But is all this real or is Dom entrapped in yet another dream? Dom uses a metal top to enable him to determine what is real and what isn't. At the end of the film, Dom spins the top. What will happen next? If the top keeps spinning, Dom is dreaming. If it falls, things are real. We don't know what happens because the ending is AMBIGUOUS.

22. UPBRAID, REPROACH, CASTIGATE:
To express disapproval; scold; rebuke;
CENSURE

In this classic scene from *Billy Madison*, Ms. Vaughn UPBRAIDS Billy for making fun of a 3rd grade student who is having trouble reading:

3rd Grader:	Wa-wa-wa-once th-th-th-th-there wa-wa-wa-was a-a-a-a g-g-girl
Billy Madison:	Kid can't even read.
Ernie:	Cut it out dude, you're gonna get us in trouble.
Billy Madison:	T-T-T-Today Junior!
Billy Madison:	OW! You're tearing my ear off!
Veronica Vaughn:	Making fun of a little kid for trying to read. Are you psycho? Do you not have a soul? You keep your mouth shut for the next two weeks or I'm going to fail you. End of story.

23. NOSTALGIA:
A sentimental longing for the past

What do the TV show *Happy Days* and the movie *Grease* have in common? Both are NOSTALGIC looks back at the 1950s when we loved Lucy, liked Ike, and wanted to be like Danny Zuko and the Fonz.

24. CONJECTURE:
An inference based upon guesswork; a SUPPOSITION

What caused the sudden extinction of the dinosaurs? Scientists have offered a number of CONJECTURES to explain why the Age of Dinosaurs came to an abrupt end. One popular CONJECTURE suggests that a giant meteor struck Mexico's Yucatan Peninsula, causing wide-spread firestorms, tidal waves, and the severe downpour of acid rain. An alternative CONJECTURE suggests that massive volcanic eruptions at the Deccan Flats in India caused climate changes that killed the dinosaurs. While both CONJECTURES are PLAUSIBLE (Word 38), scientists still lack a definitive explanation.

25. OBSOLETE, ARCHAIC, ANTIQUATED:
No longer in use; outmoded in design or style

What do the typewriter, mimeograph machine, and walkman all have in common? Although once UBIQ-UITOUS (Word 48) in offices and homes across America, all three machines are now OBSOLETE. The computer's word processing capabilities have replaced the typewriter, the high-speed photocopier has replaced the mimeograph machine, and the iPod has replaced the walkman.

26. AUSPICIOUS and PROPITIOUS:
Very favorable

How long would you wait to marry your true love? The Mogul princes of India were required to wait until the emperor's astrologers felt that all of the planetary signs were AUSPICIOUS. For example, they required Crown Prince Shah Jahan and Mumtaz Mahal to postpone their wedding date for five years. During that time, the lovers were not allowed to see one another. The long-awaited wedding finally took place when all of the astrological signs were AUSPICIOUS. The signs must have indeed been PROPITIOUS because the royal couple enjoyed nineteen years of marital joy and happiness.

27. MOROSE:
Very depressed, DESPONDENT (Word 175), mournful

During their nineteen years together, Mumtaz Mahal gave Emperor Shah Jahan fourteen children. When she suddenly died during childbirth, Shah Jahan was grief-stricken. The now MOROSE emperor canceled all appointments and refused to eat or drink for eight days. One historian recorded that when Mumtaz Mahal died, the emperor "was in danger to die himself." When he finally recovered, Shah Jahan built the Taj Mahal as a mausoleum for his beloved wife.

28. IMPASSE:
A deadlock; stalemate; failure to reach an agreement

In the movie *Avatar*, RDA is a 22nd Century company conducting mining operations on Pandora, a

VERDANT (lush, green) moon 4.37 light years from Earth. Pandora contains vast quantities of a precious mineral called unobtainium. Pandora is also home to the Na'vi, a humanoid species who live in harmony with nature. When the UNSCRUPULOUS (dishonest, unprincipled) leaders of RDA discover that the Na'vi live above a rich deposit of unobtanium, they demand that the Na'vi abandon their ancestral home. The RESOLUTE (Word 330) Na'vi refuse to leave. The IMPASSE soon leads to the outbreak of war.

29. ANACHRONISM:
The false assignment of an event, person, scene or language to a time when the event, person, scene, or word did not exist

Northern Renaissance artists often included ANA-CHRONISMS in their paintings. For example, *Last Supper* by the 15th century artist Dirk Bouts shows Christ and his disciples eating in a royal palace in what is today Belgium. While the ANACHRONISM in Bouts' painting is deliberate, the ANACHRONISMS in modern movies are unplanned blunders. For example, in the Civil War movie *Glory*, a digital watch is clearly visible on the wrist of a boy waving goodbye to the black soldiers of the 54th Massachusetts Regiment. And in the movie *Gladiator*, you can see a gas cylinder in the back of one of the overturned "Roman" chariots!

30. BELIE:
To give a false impression; to contradict

In the movie *Ten Things I Hate About You*, Kat composed a poem expressing her feelings about Patrick. As she began reading the poem to her literature class, her rhymes reflected her anger:

> *I hate the way you talk to me,*
> *And the way you cut your hair.*
> *I hate the way you drive my car.*
> *I hate it when you stare.*
> *I hate your big dumb combat boots,*
> *And the way you read my mind.*
> *I hate you so much it makes me sick;*
> *It even makes me rhyme.*

But then Kat's eyes filled with tears as she read the following lines from her poem:

> *I hate it when you're not around,*
> *And the fact that you didn't call.*
> *But mostly I hate the way I don't hate you.*
> *Not even close, not even a little bit,*
> *Not even at all.*

Kat's poem BELIED her true feelings about Patrick. Although she said she hated him, Kat actually really liked Patrick.

31. MITIGATE, MOLLIFY, ASSUAGE, ALLEVIATE:
All mean to relieve; to lessen; to ease

Did you know that almost half of all Americans take at least one prescription pill every day? Americans use pills to MITIGATE the symptoms of everything from migraine headaches to acid indigestion.

Stephen Douglas believed that the doctrine of popular sovereignty would MOLLIFY, or lessen, popular passions about the extension of slavery into the territories. But Douglas badly misjudged the public mood in the North. Instead of MOLLIFYING the public, popular sovereignty inflamed passions and helped propel the nation toward the Civil War.

32. COVET:
To strongly desire; to crave

What do Lord Voldemort (*Harry Potter and the Deathly Hallows*), The Wicked Witch of the West (*Wizard of Oz*), and Megatron (*Transformers*) all have in common? All three are villains who COVET something they can't have but desperately want. Lord Voldemort COVETS the Elder Wand, the Wicked Witch of the West COVETS Dorothy's Ruby Slippers, and Megatron COVETS the All Spark.

33. ANTITHESIS and ANTITHETICAL:
Direct opposite; the complete reverse;
ANTIPODE

In her song "You Belong With Me," Taylor Swift cannot FATHOM (understand) why a guy she likes continues to go out with a girl who is his complete ANTITHESIS. Their taste in music and sense of humor are ANTITHETICAL. But Taylor recognizes that her rival is a cheer captain who "wears short skirts" while Taylor sits in the bleachers and "wears t-shirts." All Taylor can do is hope that the guy will have an EPIPHANY (Word 298) and realize that "baby, you belong with me."

34. PROTOTYPE:
An original model

What do the Model T and the Batmobile in *Batman Begins* have in common? Although they are very different vehicles, both were originally designed to be PROTOTYPES. The Model T was invented by Henry Ford in 1908. It served as the PROTOTYPE for the world's first affordable, mass-produced automobile. The Batmobile was created by Bruce Wayne and Lucius Fox. It served as the PROTOTYPE for a series of armored cars that enabled the Caped Crusader to save Gotham from villainous criminals.

35. ALOOF:
Detached; distant physically or emotionally; reserved; standing near but apart

In *The Great Gatsby*, Fitzgerald initially portrays Jay Gatsby as the ALOOF host of lavish parties given every week at his ORNATE (Word 363) mansion. Although he is courted by powerful men and beautiful women, Gatsby chooses to remain distant and ALOOF.

In the *Iliad*, Homer states that many accused Zeus of "wanting to give victory to the Trojans." But Zeus chose to remain ALOOF: "He sat apart in his all-glorious majesty, looking down upon the Trojans, the ships of the Achaeans, the gleam of bronze, and alike upon the slayers and the slain."

36. TRITE, HACKNEYED, BANAL, PLATITUDINOUS, INSIPID:

All mean unoriginal; commonplace; overused; CLICHÉD

What are the first words that come to your mind when you think of former *American Idol* judge Paula Abdul? Most viewers remember Paula as the "nice" and AFFABLE (Word 18) judge who always said something positive about every contestant. Although Paula was nice, her comments were filled with TRITE, BANAL, and HACKNEYED phrases. According to PLATITUDINOUS Paula, every singer was "great," "beautiful," and "amazing." While Simon Cowell stung would-be singers with his CAUSTIC (Word 217) barbs, PLATITUDINOUS Paula encouraged them with pleasant but INSIPID compliments like "you're authentic," "America loves you," and "your journey of magic is just beginning."

37. ANTECEDENT:

A preceding event; a FORERUNNER; a PRECURSOR

Many critics have noted that the 1995 Disney movie *Pocahontas* can be viewed as a thematic ANTE-CEDENT to the 2010 blockbuster *Avatar*. In *Pocahontas*, AVARACIOUS (Word 229) English settlers search for gold. In *Avatar*, an AVARACIOUS (Word 229) company wanted to mine unobtanium from the fictional planet Pandora. In both movies, beautiful INDIGENOUS (Word 47) women rescue soldiers who find themselves drawn to native peoples they originally intended to conquer. By helping Captain John Smith discover the New World's life and beauty, Pocahontas serves as an ANTECEDENT for Avatar's Neytiri.

Tip for a Direct Hit

Knowing that the prefix ante means "before" can help you unlock the meaning of the words ANTEDILUVIAN and ANTEDATED. ANTE-DILUVIAN literally means "before the biblical Flood" and thus refers to anything that is extremely old and antiquated. As you can guess, ANTEDATE means to precede in time.

38.   PLAUSIBLE:
Believable; credible

IMPLAUSIBLE:
Unbelievable; incredible

Let's play PLAUSIBLE or IMPLAUSIBLE:

In the *Bourne Ultimatum*, Jason Bourne successfully breaks into Noah Vosen's heavily-guarded top security office and then steals an entire set of classified Blackbriar documents. PLAUSIBLE or IMPLAUSIBLE? PLAUSIBLE - because he is Jason Bourne!

In *Live Free or Die Hard*, John McClane successfully uses his car as a projectile to shoot down a helicopter. PLAUSIBLE or IMPLAUSIBLE? IMPLAUSIBLE - since it is Bruce Willis!

39. PRUDENT:
Careful; cautious; sensible

In the movie *Twilight*, Bella Swan is a high school student who meets and falls in love with Edward Cullen. However, Edward is not just another high school student. He is a 107 year-old vampire who stopped aging physically at 17. Edward understands that their relationship will pose grave dangers to Bella. He urges her to be PRUDENT and end their relationship. But Bella refuses to be PRUDENT and will face a future fraught with dangers.

40. AESTHETIC: *aesthetic*
Relating to what is beautiful; an appreciation of what is beautiful or attractive

In *The 40-Year-Old Virgin*, Andy's friends tell him his chest hair is not AESTHETICALLY pleasing. In order to rectify the problem, they take him to get his chest waxed. Unfortunately, the result is even uglier, or less AESTHETICALLY pleasing, than before.

41. PARADOX:
A seemingly contradictory statement that nonetheless expresses a truth

In their song "Tearin' Up My Heart," the boys from 'N Sync express a classic PARADOX:

> *It's tearin' up my heart when I'm with you*
> *But when we are apart, I feel it too*
> *And no matter what I do, I feel the pain*
> *With or without you.*

Jennifer Aniston felt the same PARADOX when she summed up how she felt about the breakup of her marriage with Brad Pitt by saying, "When you try to avoid the pain, it creates more pain."

42. ENIGMATIC and INSCRUTABLE:
Mysterious; puzzling; unfathomable; baffling

What do da Vinci's portrait the *Mona Lisa*, Fitzgerald's description of Jay Gatsby, and J.K. Rowling's portrayal of Snape have in common? All three figures are ENIGMATIC. The *Mona Lisa*'s ENIGMATIC smile has puzzled art lovers for centuries. When *The Great Gatsby* opens, Jay Gatsby is an ENIGMATIC figure whose great wealth and extravagant parties spark endless gossip. And Snape's personality and loyalties remain INSCRUTABLE until the final chapters of *Harry Potter and the Deathly Hallows*.

43. ACQUIESCE:
To comply, agree, give in

In *Pirates of the Caribbean: The Curse of the Black Pearl*, Elizabeth Swann and Captain Barbossa conduct negotiations that include "long words." Although he is a "humble pirate," Captain Barbossa does understand the meaning of the word ACQUIESCE:

> *Elizabeth Swann:* Captain Barbossa, I am here to negotiate the cessation of hostilities against Port Royal.
>
> *Captain Barbossa:* There be a lot of long words in there, Miss. We're naught but humble pirates. What is it that you want?
>
> *Elizabeth Swann:* I want you to leave and never come back.

Captain Barbossa: I'm disinclined to ACQUIESCE to your request. Means no!

In short, Captain Barbossa is NOT inclined to ACQUIESCE and comply with Elizabeth's request!

44. NAÏVE and GULLIBILE:
Unaffected simplicity; lacking worldly expertise; overly CREDULOUS; unsophisticated

What do Sandy (*Grease*), Dorothy (*Wizard of Oz*), Cady (*Mean Girls*), and Giselle (*Enchanted*) all have in common? They were all NAÏVE characters who were unsophisticated and inclined to be overly CREDULOUS. For example, Cady was originally very GULLIBLE when compared with the JADED (spoiled, overindulged) Mean Girls at North Shore High School.

45. AUTONOMOUS:
Independent; not controlled by others

In the movie *Men in Black*, Agent Zed explains that MIB is an AUTONOMOUS organization that is "not a part of the system." He goes on to say that MIB is "above the system, over it, beyond it, we are they, we are them, we are the Men in Black."

46. FUTILE:
Completely useless; doomed to failure

The Deepwater Horizon oil spill released a PRODIGIOUS (huge, massive) flood of crude oil into the Gulf of Mexico. BP engineers made repeated attempts to control or stop the spill. However, all of their initial efforts proved to be FUTILE. Although crews worked tirelessly to protect hundreds of miles of beaches, wetlands, and estuaries, local residents worried that these efforts would also prove to be FUTILE.

47. INDIGENOUS and ENDEMIC:
Both mean native to an area

Which of the following are Old World plants and animals, and which are New World plants and animals: potatoes, tomatoes, maize, sunflowers, cocoa beans, turkeys, and buffaloes? Surprisingly, all of these plants and animals are INDIGENOUS or ENDEMIC to the New World!

48. UBIQUITOUS and PREVALENT:
Characterized by being everywhere; omnipresent; widespread; PERVASIVE

What do cell phones, iPods, Starbucks coffee shops, and McDonald's fast-food restaurants have in common? They are all UBIQUITOUS - we see them everywhere. Popular fashions are also PERVASIVE. For example, baggy knee-length shorts have completely replaced the once-PREVALENT short shorts of the 1970s. From high school b-ballers to WNBA and NBA superstars, long shorts are now UBIQUITOUS.

49. PANDEMIC:
An epidemic that is geographically widespread and affects a large proportion of the population

In the movie *I Am Legend*, a man-made virus known as KV triggered a global PANDEMIC that killed almost all of the human population on Earth. While there has never been a real PANDEMIC of this magnitude, virus strains and diseases have caused widespread deaths. In 1347, the Black Plague killed as many as one-third of the people in Europe. In the 16th century, Spanish conquistadores spread small pox and other diseases that decimated the INDIGENOUS (Word 47) populations in Central America, the Caribbean, and Mexico. Our own times have not been immune to epidemics. The 1918 flu PANDEMIC killed 50 to 100 million people, and more recently we have had SARS, Asian Bird Flu, and Swine Flu PANDEMICS.

50. FORTITUDE:
Strength of mind that allows one to endure pain or adversity with courage

William Lloyd Garrison and Rosa Parks demonstrated great personal FORTITUDE by demanding an end to unjust laws. While most Americans accepted slavery, Garrison boldly demanded the immediate and unconditional emancipation of all slaves. Although initially ignored, Garrison persevered and lived to see President Lincoln issue the Emancipation Proclamation. Rosa Parks also illustrates the principle that FORTITUDE is needed to achieve difficult goals. While most Americans accepted segregation, Rosa refused a bus driver's order to give up her seat to a white passenger. Her historic action helped GALVANIZE (Word 148) the Civil Rights Movement.

Testing Your Vocabulary

Each SAT contains 19 sentence completion questions that are primarily a test of your vocabulary. Each sentence completion will always have a key word or phrase that will lead you to the correct answer. Use the vocabulary from Chapter 1 to circle the answer to each of the following 10 sentence completion questions. You'll find answers and explanations on pages 30 to 31.

1. In contrast to the clandestine maneuvers of her associates, Crystal's methods were always open and _____.

   (A) aesthetic
   (B) painstaking
   (C) nostalgic
   (D) aloof
   (E) aboveboard

2. Cell phones seem to be _____, so prevalent are they that they seem to be everywhere.

   (A) anomalies
   (B) anachronistic
   (C) ubiquitous
   (D) autonomous
   (E) obsolete

3. Paradoxically, this successful politician is sometimes very sociable and other times very _____.

    (A) aloof
    (B) genial
    (C) trite
    (D) pragmatic
    (E) naïve

4. Uncertainty is an unavoidable part of the stock market; investors should, therefore, learn to accept doubt and tolerate _____.

    (A) futility
    (B) pragmatism
    (C) diffidence
    (D) ambiguity
    (E) sarcasm

5. Paleontologists like China's Xu Xing now find themselves in the _____ situation of using state-of-the art equipment to analyze prehistoric fossils.

    (A) futile
    (B) nostalgic
    (C) coveted
    (D) paradoxical
    (E) banal

6. Since all the economic indicators were favorable, it seemed like _____ time to begin the long-awaited project.

    (A) an ambiguous
    (B) an auspicious
    (C) an implausible
    (D) a futile
    (E) a clandestine

7. General MacArthur's bold disregard for popular conventions and time-honored military strategies earned him a reputation for _____.

    (A) acquiescence
    (B) audacity
    (C) prudence
    (D) indifference
    (E) ambivalence

8. The scientist was both _____ and _____: she was always careful to test each hypothesis and cautious not to jump to conclusions.

    (A) painstaking .. despondent
    (B) nostalgic .. sentimental
    (C) clandestine .. unconventional
    (D) recalcitrant .. presumptuous
    (E) meticulous .. prudent

9. Mischa admired his grandparents' _____:
   during the Great Depression they lost their jobs,
   but they never lost their strength of purpose or
   their dignity.

   (A) fortitude
   (B) antecedents
   (C) anomalies
   (D) indifference
   (E) diffidence

10. Parker's _____ nature, evident in his stubborn
    refusal to follow instructions, exasperated and
    _____ his teammates and coaches.

    (A) morose .. mollified
    (B) obdurate .. charmed
    (C) sarcastic .. calmed
    (D) genial .. annoyed
    (E) recalcitrant .. alienated

Answers and Explanations

1. **E**

   The question asks you to find a word that contrasts with clandestine and is synonymous with open. The correct answer is ABOVEBOARD (Word 17).

2. **C**

   The question asks you to find a word that means prevalent. The correct answer is UBIQUITOUS (Word 48).

3. **A**

   The question asks you to find a word that is the opposite of sociable. The correct answer is ALOOF (Word 35).

4. **D**

   The question asks you to find a word that means uncertain and fits with the phrase "accept doubt." The correct answer is AMBIGUITY (Word 21).

5. **D**

   The question asks you to find a word that satisfies the contradictory but true situation in which Xu Xing uses state-of-the art equipment to analyze prehistoric fossils. The correct answer is PARADOXICAL (Word 41).

6. B

The question asks you to find a word that means favorable. The correct answer is AUSPICIOUS (Word 26).

7. B

The question asks you to find a word that means a bold disregard for popular conventions and time-honored military strategies. The correct answer is AUDACITY (Word 9).

8. E

The question asks you to find a first word that means careful and a second word that means cautious. Note that in choice A, painstaking does mean careful, but despondent means very depressed. The correct answers are MET-ICULOUS (Word 8) and PRUDENT (Word 39).

9. A

The question asks you to find a word that means strength of purpose. The correct answer is FORTITUDE (Word 50).

10. E

The question asks you to find a first word that means stubborn refusal to follow instructions and a second word that is synonymous with exasperate. Note that in choice B, obdurate does mean stubborn, but Parker's teammates would not be charmed. The correct answers are RECALCITRANT (Word 15) and ALIENATED.

Chapter 2

CORE VOCABULARY II: 51–100

Chapter 2 continues our goal of helping you learn the 100 Core Vocabulary Words. As in Chapter 1, each of these words was the answer to a Level 3 or Level 4 question. We EXHORT (strongly encourage) you to study hard. As always, our PENCHANT (liking) for vivid pop culture examples will help you learn and remember new words. So don't let the Core Words THWART (frustrate) you. Now is the time to TENACIOUSLY (with great determination) pursue your goal of conquering the SAT. Remember, there is INCONTROVERTIBLE (indisputable) proof that your Critical Reading score will go up as your vocabulary goes up!

51. DIMINUTIVE:
Very small

Jersey Shore's Nicole "Snookie" Polizzi is just 4' 9" tall. The DIMINUTUVE reality star piles her long dark hair into a towering bob to create an illusion of greater height. The DIMINUTIVE Snookie proudly boasts that her hair is real, saying "there's no extensions, sweeties. Every girl's trying to copy my pouf!"

52. TRIVIAL and MINUTIAE:
Trifling; unimportant; insignificant; minor everyday details

Drake is one of the world's most popular hip hop artists. While Drake would prefer to concentrate on creating music, his zealous fans often focus on interesting but TRIVIAL MINUTIAE about his personal life. For example, Drake was raised by a Jewish mother and had a Bar Mitzvah. And online rumors continue to link him with Rihanna!

53. EXHORT:
To encourage; urge; IMPLORE; give a pep talk

Are you a member of a team? If so, has your coach ever given your team a pep talk designed to EXHORT you to give it 110 percent and win the game? Taken from the movie *Braveheart*, here is William Wallace's famous speech EXHORTING the Scottish troops to stand and fight the English:

William Wallace: What will you do without freedom? Will you fight?

Soldier:	Against that? No, we will run, and we will live.
William Wallace:	Aye, fight and you may die. Run, and you'll live. At least for a while. And dying in your beds, many years from now, would you be willing to trade all the days, from this day to that, for one chance, just one chance to come back and tell our enemies that they may take our lives, but they'll never take OUR FREEDOM!

54. ANTIPATHY, ANIMOSITY, RANCOR:
Strong dislike; ill will; the state of DETESTING someone; ENMITY

In the TV show *Glee*, Will Schuster is a GENIAL (Word 18) Spanish teacher who wants to revive his high school's MORIBUND (Word 331) glee club. In addition to recruiting and coaching new performers, Will must also overcome the relentless ANIMOSITY of Sue Sylvester, the egotistical head coach of the school's championship cheerleading team. Sue's repeated attempts to SABOTAGE (undermine) Will create a RANCOROUS relationship between the two rival coaches.

55. DIGRESS:
To depart from a subject; wander; ramble

Have you ever listened to someone who repeatedly wanders off a topic? If so, then you know how confusing and annoying it is when a speaker DIGRESSES from a subject. For example, in the movie, *Office Space*, Milton is notorious for his long-winded DIGRESSIONS (See Word 5). DIGRESSING from a topic is not limited to speaking. Writers sometimes DIGRESS or wander off a topic. On the SAT I, your first task will be to write an essay. Readers reward essays that are well-organized and deduct points from essays that DIGRESS from the topic.

Tip for a Direct Hit

DIGRESS contains the Latin root *gress*, meaning "to step." So DIGRESS literally means to step away (*di*) or depart from a topic. You can also see *gress* in progress, to step forward (*pro*), regress, to step back (*re*), and transgress, to step across (*trans*). Committing a transgression literally means to step across a line that divides right from wrong.

56. TENACIOUS:
Characterized by holding fast; showing great determination in holding on to something that is valued

What do Jason Bourne (*The Bourne Ultimatum*), Noah Calhoun (*The Notebook*), and Jamal Malik (*Slumdog Millionaire*) have in common? All three TENACIOUSLY pursued something they desperately wanted. Jason Bourne refused to accept the loss of his identity. He showed great TENACITY in his single-minded attempt to learn who he was. Noah Calhoun loved and lost Allie. He then demonstrated great TENACITY in his attempt to win her back. And finally, Jamal refused to accept being separated from Latika. He demonstrated great TENACITY in his attempts to find her.

57. INDULGENT:
Characterized by excessive generosity; overly tolerant

In the movie *Mean Girls*, Regina George's mother prides herself on being INDULGENT. She proudly tells Regina and Cady, "I just want you to know, if you ever need anything, don't be shy, OK? There are NO rules in the house. I'm not like a 'regular' mom. I'm a 'cool' mom." Mrs. George should have said, "I'm a super-INDULGENT mom who lets Regina do anything she wishes."

58. DIVISIVE and POLARIZE:
Both mean to create disunity or dissension; to break up into opposing factions or groups

Americans have a long and distinguished record of settling differences by reaching a compromise. However, some issues are so POLARIZING that a compromise is impossible. Before the Civil War, the issue of slavery POLARIZED Americans into two groups: those who defended the South's "peculiar institution" and those who demanded that slavery be abolished. Lincoln eloquently expressed this division when he said, "A house divided against itself cannot stand. I believe this government cannot endure permanently half slave and half free."

59. NEBULOUS:
Vague; cloudy; misty; lacking a fully developed form

Have you read the Epilogue in *Harry Potter and the Deathly Hallows*? If you found it rather vague, then J.K. Rowling achieved her goal. In an interview, Rowling stated that the Epilogue is deliberately "NEBULOUS." She wanted readers to feel as if they were looking at Platform 9 3/4 through the mist, unable to make out exactly who was there and who was not.

60. ANALOGY and ANALOGOUS:
A similarity or likeness

Did you know that for most of its history the SAT I included a number of ANALOGY questions? For example, students were asked to see the ANALOGY or similarity between a tree and a forest and a star and a galaxy. The ANALOGY is that a tree is part of a forest in the same way that a star is part of a galaxy. Although the College Board removed analogies in 2005, SAT I test writers still expect students to recognize analogies in critical readings. Don't let the phrase "is most ANALOGOUS to" confuse you. The question is asking you to identify a situation or example that is most similar to the one in the reading passage.

61. FLEETING and EPHEMERAL:
Both mean very brief; lasting for a short time

What do the following groups and their hit songs have in common: "Who Let the Dogs Out?" by Baha Men, "Stuck In The Middle With You" by Stealers Wheel, and "It's Raining Men" by the Weather Girls? All three groups were "one-hit wonders" who had a single hit song and then disappeared. Their popularity was FLEETING. They were EPHEMERAL - here today and gone tomorrow.

predilection

62. PENCHANT and PREDILECTION:
Both mean a *liking or preference for something; an INCLINATION*

What do film star Angelina Jolie and rap artist Lil Wayne have in common? Both have a well-known PENCHANT for tattoos. Angelina's tattoos include a prayer of Buddhist Sanskrit symbols to honor her first adopted son Maddox, coordinates representing the geographic locations of her children's birthplaces, and the statement "know your rights." Lil Wayne's PREDILECTION for tattoos has led him to cover his face and torso with tattoos. For example, a red tattoo above his right eyebrow states, "I am music," emphasizing Lil Wayne's love of music. The numbers 9 27 82 on his right forearm are his date of birth.

63. CAPRICIOUS and MERCURIAL:
Very changeable; fickle; characterized by constantly-shifting moods

In 2008, tweenage girls COVETED (Word 32) tickets to attend sold-out concerts featuring the Jonas Brothers. The young fans shrieked with delight as the "Joe Bros" sang their hit song "Burning Up." But pop music fans are CAPRICIOUS. Kevin's marriage fueled speculation that the Jonas Brothers' popularity had begun to WANE (decline). For example, the 2010 Jonas Brother concert tour with Demi Lovato was originally scheduled to visit 45 North American cities. However, sluggish ticket sales forced promoters to reduce the tour to 29 cities. Meanwhile, MERCURIAL tweenage girls had just two words to explain the decline of the Jonas Brothers – Justin Bieber.

64. BOORISH, UNCOUTH, CRASS:

Vulgar; characterized by crude behavior and deplorable manners; unrefined

Billy Madison (*Billy Madison*), Ron Burgundy (*Anchorman*), Borat (*Borat*), and Ben Stone (*Knocked Up*) all demonstrated BOORISH manners and behaviors. However, none of these UNCOUTH characters quite equaled Bluto in *Animal House*. In a classic scene, Bluto piled food onto his cafeteria plate while stuffing food in his pockets. He then sat down uninvited at a cafeteria table. Disgusted by Bluto's outrageous appearance and CRASS manners, Mandy called him a "P-I-G, pig." Undeterred by Mandy's insult, Bluto stuffed mashed potatoes into his mouth and asked Mandy and her INCREDULOUS (disbelieving) friends, "Can you guess what I am?" He then pressed his hands against his cheeks, causing the mashed potatoes to spray onto the shocked diners. Pleased with his BOORISH antics, Bluto proudly answered his own question by announcing, "I'm a zit, get it!"

65. INDIGNANT:

Characterized by outrage at something that is perceived as unjust

What do Andrew Jackson's supporters in 1824 and Al Gore's supporters in 2000 have in common? Both were INDIGNANT at the outcomes of presidential elections. Following the election of 1824, Andrew Jackson's INDIGNANT supporters accused John Quincy Adams and Henry Clay of stealing the election from Old Hickory. Following the election of 2000, Al Gore's INDIGNANT supporters accused George W. Bush and the U.S. Supreme Court of stealing the election from Gore.

66. INNUENDO:
A veiled reference; an insinuation

Celebrity magazines and gossip bloggers thrive on using INNUENDOES to spark interest and stir up controversy. Kristen Stewart and Rob Pattinson are stars of the hit *Twilight* movies. *Us Weekly* placed a picture of Kristen and Rob on their cover next to the headline: "Twilight Love Trouble – Why She'll Break His Heart." Although the story lacked documented facts, it nonetheless featured INNUENDOES by "sources close to the couple." For example, one "Pattinson insider" told *Us Weekly*, "He's obsessed with Kristen, totally obsessed." But their "tortured romance" is based on Kristen's CAPRICIOUS (Word 63) moods. "When Kristen is happy, they're happy, but when she is not, watch out."

67. THWART and STYMIE:
To stop, frustrate, prevent

The Harry Potter saga is filled with dramatic examples illustrating THWART and STYMIE. For example, Lily Potter's love THWARTED Lord Voldemort's attempt to kill her one-year-old son Harry. In future volumes,

Harry repeatedly THWARTED Lord Voldemort's attempts to kill him.

68. ADROIT, DEFT, ADEPT:
To have or show great skill; DEXTEROUS; nimble

What do teenager Kate Moore and action star Chuck Norris have in common? Kate has DEXTEROUS hands, and Chuck has ADROIT legs. Let me explain! Kate is the U.S. National Texting Champion. She beat out 20 other finalists by DEFTLY texting blindfolded and while maneuvering through a moving obstacle course. As everyone knows, Chuck Norris is ADEPT at using a roundhouse kick to escape even the toughest situations. In fact, it is rumored that if someone were DEFT enough to tap the energy from a Chuck Norris roundhouse kick, he or she could power the entire country of Australia for 44 minutes.

 Tip for a Direct Hit

Are you right-handed or left-handed? Right-handed people were once thought to be more ADROIT and DEXTEROUS than left-handed people. This bias can be seen in the etymology of these two words. The English word ADROIT is actually derived from the French word *droit* meaning right, as opposed to left. So if you are MALADROIT, you are not skillful. The ancient Romans shared the same positive view of right-handed people. The Latin word *dexter* means right, as opposed to left.

---

69. ADMONISH:
To earnestly caution; to warn against (another) to avoid a course of action

First sung in November 1934, "Santa Claus is Coming to Town" celebrates Santa's much anticipated arrival on Christmas Eve. However, while Santa may be very MUNIFICENT (Word 232), he is also very VIGILANT (watchful, alert). He keeps a list and he knows "who's naughty or nice." The song earnestly ADMONISHES children to "be good for goodness sake."

70. INCONTROVERTIBLE:
Indisputable; beyond doubt

As the movie *Harry Potter and the Order of the Phoenix* opens, Albus Dumbledore emphatically tells Cornelius Fudge and other Ministry of Magic officials that "the evidence of the Dark Lord's return is IN-CONTROVERTIBLE." Unfortunately, Fudge, Dolores Umbridge, and other officials are SKEPTICAL (Word 102). Needless to say, as the story unfolds, it is clear that Dumbledore is correct and Fudge is ERRONEOUS (Word 192).

71. VORACIOUS and RAVENOUS:
A huge appetite that cannot be satisfied; INSATIABLE

What do Homer (*The Simpsons*), Bluto (*Animal House*), and Galactus (*Fantastic Four: Rise of the Silver Surfer*) have in common? All three have VORACIOUS appetites. Homer has an INSATIABLE appetite for frosted doughnuts. Bluto regularly piles great quantities of food on his plate. And Galactus is a cosmic entity who has a RAVENOUS appetite for planets like Earth that have the potential for supporting life.

72. CALLOUS:
Emotionally hardened; insensitive; unfeeling

In the movie *Mean Girls*, the Plastics CALLOUSLY mistreated their classmates. They even kept a "Burn Book" filled with CALLOUS INNUENDOES (Word 66) and SARCASTIC (Word 3) putdowns.

In Fitzgerald's novel *The Great Gatsby*, Tom Buchanan CALLOUSLY ruins four lives (Daisy, Gatsby, Myrtle, and George) while recklessly pursuing his own selfish pleasures.

73. INTREPID and UNDAUNTED:
Both mean courageous, resolute, and fearless

What do Luke Skywalker and Charles Lindbergh have in common? Both were INTREPID pilots who were UNDAUNTED by seemingly impossible odds. In the movie *Star Wars: Episode IV*, Luke was UNDAUNTED by the Empire's seemingly invincible Death Star. The INTREPID Skywalker destroyed the Death Star with well-aimed proton torpedoes.

The American aviator Charles Lindbergh was also UNDAUNTED by a seemingly impossible task. Despite several attempts, no pilot had successfully flown across the Atlantic. In 1927, the INTREPID Lindbergh electrified the world by flying his single-engine plane, the *Spirit of St. Louis*, from New York to Paris in a grueling 33-hour and 39-minute flight.

74. NONCHALANT:

Having an air of casual indifference; coolly unconcerned

When you are driving, do you slow down for a yellow light and promptly stop for a red light? We hope so. While careful and law-abiding drivers follow these rules of the road, not all drivers do. For example, Italian drivers are famous for their NONCHALANT attitude toward yellow and even red lights. One typical Italian cab driver NONCHALANTLY explained that lights are merely advisory: "Everyone drives through yellow lights and fresh red ones. It is no big deal." Needless to say, we hope you will not take such a NONCHALANT attitude.

75. CONVOLUTED:

Winding, twisting, and therefore difficult to understand; intricate

What do the Electoral College and the Bowl Championship Series (BCS) have in common? Both require a CONVOLUTED process to choose a winner. The Electoral College requires a CONVOLUTED process to choose a President, and the BCS requires a CONVOLUTED process to choose two football teams to play for the national championship.

76. ITINERANT:

Traveling from place to place; NOT SEDENTARY

During the Great Awakening, George Whitefield and other ITINERANT ministers preached their message of human helplessness and divine OMNIPOTENCE (all-powerful) as they toured the colonies. Today, many movie stars also live ITINERANT lives. For example, during the last six years, Angelina Jolie and Brad Pitt have lived in 15 homes all over the world, including Paris, Prague, Los Angeles, New Orleans, Berlin, Namibia, India, and New York City. Jolie enjoys her ITINERANT lifestyle and says that it is important to experience a variety of cultures.

77. POIGNANT:
Moving; touching; heartrending

In the movie *Remember the Titans*, Gerry Bertier and Julius Campbell are forced to become teammates on the racially divided T.C. Williams High School football team. Although originally bitter rivals, they overcome their prejudices and become close friends. Do you remember the POIGNANT scene in *Remember the Titans* when Julius visited the paralyzed Gerry in the hospital? At first, the nurse refused to allow Julius, who was black, to enter the room saying, "Only kin's allowed in here." But Gerry corrected her saying, "Alice, are you blind? Don't you see the family resemblance? That's my brother." This POIGNANT scene brought tears to the eyes of many viewers.

78. IMPETUS:
A stimulus or encouragement that results in increased activity

Lord Voldemort's resurrection at the end of *Harry Potter and the Goblet of Fire* provided the IMPETUS for the revival of the Order of the Phoenix and the formation of Dumbledore's Army.

Although it was a failure, Shays' Rebellion alarmed key colonial leaders, thus providing the IMPETUS for calling a convention to revise and strengthen the Articles of Confederation.

79. BUCOLIC, RUSTIC, PASTORAL:
All of these words refer to charming, unspoiled countryside

Americans have always been proud of our country's great natural beauty. During the early 19th century, a group of artists known as the Hudson River School specialized in painting the RUSTIC beauty of America's unspoiled landscape. Today, many students are attracted to the PASTORAL beauty of campuses located in small towns. For example, one writer described Blacksburg, Virginia, the home of Virginia Tech, as "a quaint, off-the-beaten-track, BUCOLIC college town nestled in the mountains of southwest Virginia."

equanimity   *unflappable*

80. EQUANIMITY and UNFLAPPABLE:
Calmness; composure; even-tempered; poise

As US Airways Flight 1549 climbed into the sky above New York City, everything seemed normal. Then, just 1 minute 37 seconds after takeoff, the plane struck a flock of Canadian geese, disabling both engines. Captain Chesley Sullenberger quickly decided that he only had one option – to land the plane and its 150 passengers in the frigid waters of the Hudson River. Despite the intense pressure, Captain Sullenberger maintained his EQUANIMITY. He calmly told the air traffic controller, "We're going to be in the Hudson" and then alerted passengers to "brace for impact."

Still maintaining his calm demeanor, the UNFLAPPABLE "Captain Cool" smoothly ditched the plane in the river. Everyone on board survived.

81. PANACHE, VERVE, FLAMBOYANT:
Great vigor and energy; dash, especially in artistic performance and composition

During the Middle Ages, proud European military commanders often placed feathers or a plume in their helmets as they rode into battle. Known as a *panache*, the feathers and plumes helped troops identify their commander while also making him an easier target for enemy arrows and bullets. Given the risk, it took real courage for a commander to wear a *panache*.

Today the word PANACHE no longer refers to feathers or a plume. But PANACHE still retains its sense of VERVE or dash. PANACHE is now most frequently used to refer to FLAMBOYANT entertainers. For example, Lady Gaga is one of the music world's most FLAMBOYANT performers.

82. PROVOCATIVE:
Provoking discussion and stimulating controversy

Prior to World War I, young women aspired to seem modest and maidenly. But that changed during the Roaring Twenties. Once DEMURE (modest) maidens now PROVOCATIVELY proclaimed their new freedom by becoming "flappers." Flappers shocked their elders by dancing the Charleston and wearing one-piece bathing suits. Dismayed by this PROVOCATIVE clothing, officials at some beaches insisted on measuring the length of the bathing suits to make sure that they did not reveal too much of the women's legs. In today's world, this notion of PROVOCATIVE would seem ARCHAIC (Word 25)!

83. PLACID:
Calm or quiet; undisturbed by tumult or disorder; SERENE

What do the Pacific Ocean and the SAT word PLACID have in common? When the legendary explorer Ferdinand Magellan left the Strait of Magellan, he entered an immense and as yet unexplored body of water that he described as a *Mare Pacificum*, or "peaceful sea." The Latin root *plac* means to make calm. Since the SAT word PLACID also contains this root, it too means to be calm or quiet.

84. FORTUITOUS:
Of accidental but fortunate occurrence; having unexpected good fortune

In the fall of 1862, the South appeared to be on the verge of victory in the Civil War. Following a brilliant triumph at the Second Battle of Bull Run, General Lee boldly invaded Maryland. In war, however, decisive battles are often determined as much by a FORTU-ITOUS accident as by a carefully planned strategy. As Lee's army steadily advanced, a Union corporal discovered a bulky envelope lying in the grass near a shade tree. Curious, he picked it up and discovered three cigars wrapped in a piece of paper containing Lee's secret battle plans. This FORTUITOUS dis-covery played a key role in enabling the Union forces to win a pivotal victory at the Battle of Antietam.

85. DISPEL:
To drive away; scatter; as to DISPEL a misconception

Most football coaches believe that you have to yell and scream at your players in order to win. However, Tony Dungy, the former Head Coach of the Indianapolis Colts, disagrees. In his book *Quiet Strength*, Dungy DISPELS this misconception. Dungy does not belittle his players or scream at them. Instead, he talks quietly and treats everyone with respect. He guides his players instead of goading them.

86. AMALGAM: amalgam
A mixture; blend, combination of different elements

Rap star Ludacris' name is actually an AMALGAM. He combined his birth name Cris and his radio handle Luda to COIN (Word 269) the new name – LUDACRIS!

Similarly, rap star Jay-Z's name is also an AMAL-GAM. Shawn Carter grew up in Brooklyn near where the J-Z subway line has a stop on Marcy Avenue. Carter's friends nicknamed him "Jazzy." Carter later combined the name of the subway line with his nick-name to COIN the new name Jay-Z!

87. VIABLE and FEASIBLE:
Both mean capable of being accomplished; possible

Soaring oil costs and worries about global warming have prompted a search for VIABLE alternatives to gasoline. Many believe that biofuels, such as corn ethanol, are the most FEASIBLE alternative to America's dependence upon imported oil. Indeed, investments in biofuels soared from $5 billion in 1995 to $38 billion in 2005 and are expected to top $110 billion in 2010. But critics argue that corn ethanol is neither VIABLE nor cost-effective. By diverting grain from dinner plates to fuel tanks, biofuels are raising world food prices. The grain it takes to fill an SUV tank with ethanol could feed a person for a year.

88. ANGUISH:
Agonizing physical or mental pain; torment

The movie *Batman Begins* opens with a young boy's ANGUISH. Eight-year-old Bruce Wayne falls into a cave, where he encounters a swarm of bats. Bruce develops a fear of bats and later urges his parents to leave an opera featuring bat-like creatures. Outside the theater, Bruce's parents are both killed in a robbery. Filled with ANGUISH, Bruce blames himself for his parents' murder and dedicates himself to seeking revenge by fighting the criminals who control Gotham City. As the Caped Crusader, Batman, Bruce wages a successful fight against crime but must face new and even more ANGUISHING questions: Does his crusade have an end? Can he ever have an ordinary life?

89. INTEMPERATE:
Lacking restraint; excessive

TEMPERATE:
Exercising moderation and restraint

INTEMPERATE habits such as smoking, drinking, and overeating are INIMICAL (harmful) to good health. In contrast, a TEMPERATE person leads a lifestyle characterized by moderation and self-restraint. Bluto (*Animal House*), Frank "The Tank" (*Old School*), and Ben Stone (*Knocked Up*) were all fun-loving, INTEMPERATE party animals. Compare them with Andy Stitzer's (*The 40-Year-Old Virgin*) far more TEMPERATE approach to life.

90. SUPERFICIAL:
Shallow; lacking in depth; concerned with surface appearances

What do Cher (*Clueless*) and Daisy Buchanan (*The Great Gatsby*) have in common? Both were SUPERFICIAL. In *Clueless*, Josh called Cher "a SUPERFICIAL space cadet" because she lacked direction. Daisy proved to be a SUPERFICIAL person who prized material possessions. For example, she burst into tears when Gatsby showed her his collection of English dress shirts. Gatsby would tragically discover that beneath Daisy's SUPER-FICIAL surface there was only more surface.

91. LAUD, EXTOL, TOUT, ACCLAIM:
All mean to praise; applaud

What do the Beach Boys' classic song "California Girls" and Katy Perry's hit "California Gurls" have in common? Well duh! Both songs EXTOL the beauty of California girls. The Beach Boys acknowledge that they are BEGUILED (enticed, captivated) by the way southern girls talk. They LAUD east coast girls for being hip. However, this doesn't shake their CONVICTION (firm belief) that California girls are "the cutest girls in the world."

Concurs

Needless to say, Katy Perry CONCURS (agrees) with the Beach Boys. She proudly TOUTS the beauty of California's ACCLAIMED golden coast. But that is not all. The California boys "break their necks" trying to sneak a peek at the VOLUPTUOUS (very sensual) "California gurls." And who can blame them? According to Katy, "California gurls" are "unforgettable, Daisy Dukes, bikinis on top."

Tip for a Direct Hit

LAUDS is the morning Church service in which psalms of praise to God are sung. Note that the word appLAUD contains the root word LAUD. LAUD and its synonyms EXTOL, TOUT, and ACCLAIM all mean to praise.

92. DISMISSIVE:
Showing INDIFFERENCE (Word 10) or disregard; to reject

What do the artist Jackson Pollock, the author J.K. Rowling, and the reggae singer and rapper Sean Kingston have in common? All three had to overcome DISMISSIVE critics. Bewildered critics ridiculed Pollock, calling him "Jack the Dripper." INDIFFERENT (Word 10) editors at numerous publishing houses rejected J.K. Rowling's story about a boy wizard named Harry Potter. And Sean Kingston almost quit the music industry after his idols Timbaland and Pharrel dismissed his early recordings.

93. DISPARAGE:

To speak of in a slighting or disrespectful way; belittle

Did you see the movie *Transformers: Revenge of the Fallen*? If so, what was your opinion of the movie? Does it deserve to be LAUDED (Word 91) or DISPARAGED? You might be surprised to learn that Megan Fox, the actress who played Mikaela Banes, DISPARAGED *Transformers* director Michael Bay for focusing more on special effects than acting. Fox also blasted Bay calling him a dictator "who wants to be like Hitler on his sets." GALLED (irked) by Fox's DISPARAGING remarks, Bay shot back saying that Fox is young, "and has a lot of growing to do." Bay finally ended the war of words when he cut Fox from "Transformers 3" saying her role was not INTEGRAL (essential) to the story.

94. POMPOUS:

Filled with excessive self-importance; pretentious

In the Harry Potter SAGA (Word 208), Draco Malfoy is a POMPOUS bully who arrogantly proclaims that pure-blood wizards are far superior to Muggles (non-wizards) and especially Mudbloods (Muggle-born witches and wizards). The POMPOUS Malfoy loves to use verbal taunts to DENIGRATE (malign) Harry, Ron, and Hermione. J.K. Rowling uses Draco as a literary FOIL (contrast) to her modest hero, Harry Potter.

95. CRYPTIC:
Having a hidden or AMBIGUOUS (Word 21) meaning; mysterious

As *Harry Potter and the Chamber of Secrets* opens, Dobby delivers this CRYPTIC message to Harry: "Harry Potter must not go back to Hogwarts." But why must Harry stay away from Hogwarts? We don't know, because the message is CRYPTIC. Later in the same book, this CRYPTIC message appears on one of the walls at Hogwarts: "The Chamber of Secrets has been opened. Enemies of the Heir, Beware." Once again, since the message is CRYPTIC, we are not sure what it means.

96. SUBTLE:
A gradual change that is difficult to detect immediately

In the movie *Clueless*, Josh and Cher initially appear to dislike each other. In fact, Josh calls Cher a "SUPERFICIAL (Word 90) space cadet" and criticizes her for lacking direction. However, as the movie unfolds, there is a SUBTLE change in their relationship as they slowly become closer and closer. In the movie *Billy Madison*, a similar SUBTLE change occurs between Veronica Vaughn and Billy Madison. In the beginning, Ms. Vaughn detests Billy for his immature behavior. However, as Billy gradually matures, he begins to win Veronica's respect.

97. DISPARITY:
An inequality; a gap; an imbalance

Mumbai is India's financial capital and largest city. The movie *Slumdog Millionaire* featured vivid images of the DISPARITY in housing between the wealthy few who live in the city's luxury condominiums and the poverty-stricken masses who live in tiny shacks in the densely crowded Dharavi slum.

 Tip for a Direct Hit

DISPARITY contains the Latin root *par* meaning "that which is equal." The root still lives in the golfing term *"par"* which means to be equal to the course. It can also be seen in the SAT word PARITY which means equal in status or value.

98. CURTAIL:
To cut short or reduce

The Gulf Oil Spill created an UNPRECEDENTED (Word 259) environmental and economic disaster. As a toxic oil slick spread across the Gulf's once PRISTINE (Word 383) beaches and wetlands, EXASPERATED (angry, frustrated) workers lost jobs while worried tourists CURTAILED and even cancelled vacation trips to the region. The spill underscored America's dependence upon gasoline. On average, Americans consume about 386 million gallons of gasoline each day. This PRODIGIOUS (huge) rate of consumption cannot go on forever. Many PUNDITS (Word 117) argue that Americans must CURTAIL their fuel consumption by developing renewable sources of energy.

99. INNOCUOUS:

Harmless; not likely to give offense or to arouse strong feelings or hostility

Have you ever invited your boyfriend or girlfriend to meet your parents? If so, then you know that there is no such thing as an INNOCUOUS question or answer. For example, in the movie *The Notebook*, Allie invites Noah to meet her upper-class parents and some of their wealthy friends. One friend asks Noah what he does for a living. Noah replies that he earns 40 cents an hour working at the local lumberyard. That's not bad for a young man in 1940. But Noah's seemingly INNOCUOUS answer alarms Allie's socially-conscious mother. She concludes that Noah is not good enough for her daughter and that their summer romance must end.

100. DIATRIBE and TIRADE:

A bitter abusive denunciation; a thunderous verbal attack

What do Coach Carter (*Coach Carter*), Coach Gaines (*Friday Night Lights*), and Coach Boone (*Remember the Titans*) all have in common? All three coaches were passionate about building character and team-work. And, if necessary, all three didn't hesitate to deliver a TIRADE when a player failed to follow team rules or perform to the best of his ability. For example, Coach Boone demanded perfection. In one memorable DIATRIBE he insisted, "We will be perfect in every aspect of the game. You drop a pass, you run a mile. You miss a blocking assignment, you run a mile. You fumble the football, and I will break my foot off in your John Brown hind pants and then you will run a mile. Perfection. Let's go to work!"

Testing Your Vocabulary

Each SAT contains 19 sentence completion questions that are primarily a test of your vocabulary. Each sentence completion will always have a key word or phrase that will lead you to the correct answer. Use the vocabulary from Chapters 1 and 2 to circle the answer to each of the following 10 sentence completion questions. You'll find answers and explanations on pages 62 to 63.

1.   After his long, exhausting swim, Rajon was _____: he wanted to eat until he could eat no more.

    (A)   callous
    (B)   pompous
    (C)   presumptuous
    (D)   voracious
    (E)   capricious

2.   Serena Williams is often described as having _____ that is apparent in both her dazzling tennis performances and her flamboyant athletic-wear designs.

    (A)   an equanimity
    (B)   a panache
    (C)   a superficiality
    (D)   a nonchalance
    (E)   a subtlety

3.   Instead of presenting a balanced view of both sides of the issue, the speaker became increasingly _____, insisting that her opponents were both factually inaccurate and morally wrong.

(A)   enigmatic
(B)   indignant
(C)   ravenous
(D)   placid
(E)   innocuous

4.   The Post-Modern architectural style is _____: it combines diverse elements, including classical columns, Baroque ornamentation, and Palladian windows.

(A)   a diatribe
(B)   a conjecture
(C)   an impasse
(D)   an anachronism
(E)   an amalgam

5.   The _____ message baffled experts who were unable to decipher its ambiguous meaning.

(A)   archaic
(B)   poignant
(C)   cryptic
(D)   dismissive
(E)   fleeting

6.   Boisterous, uncouth, and devoid of all manners, Artem was widely known for his _____ behavior.

(A)   boorish
(B)   intrepid
(C)   subtle
(D)   temperate
(E)   laudable

7.   The coach's halftime speech to his team was a _____, a bitter railing denouncing their inept play.

(A)   diatribe
(B)   conjecture
(C)   innuendo
(D)   evocation
(E)   antecedent

8.   Hira's supervisor faulted her for turning in a _____ proposal that was overly vague and lacked a detailed analysis of costs and benefits.

(A)   morose
(B)   pompous
(C)   nebulous
(D)   viable
(E)   polarizing

9. The new zoning ordinance provoked such intense debate and caused such partisanship that it was branded the most _____ in the community's long history.

    (A)   innocuous
    (B)   subtle
    (C)   superficial
    (D)   archaic
    (E)   divisive

10. Emily was renowned for her _____; she remained calm and composed even when confronted with stressful personal problems.

    (A)   callousness
    (B)   capriciousness
    (C)   intemperance
    (D)   equanimity
    (E)   superficiality

Answers and Explanations

1.   **D**

The question asks you to find a word that is consistent with the phrase "he wanted to eat until he could eat no more." The correct answer is VORACIOUS (Word 71) because a person with a voracious appetite is INSATIABLE.

2.   **B**

The question asks you to find a word that means "dazzling" and "flamboyant." The correct answer is PANACHE (Word 81).

3.   **B**

The question asks you to find a word that is consistent with the phrase "insisting that her opponents were both factually inaccurate and morally wrong." The correct answer is IND-IGNANT (Word 65) because someone who is INDIGNANT is outraged by something that is unjust and morally wrong.

4.   **E**

The question asks you to find a word that means "combines diverse elements." The correct answer is AMALGAM (Word 86).

5.   **C**

The question asks you to find a word that would baffle experts because of its "ambiguous meaning." The correct answer is CRYPTIC (Word 95), because a CRYPTIC message is mysterious and would therefore baffle experts with its ambiguous meaning.

6.   A

The question asks you to find a word that means "boisterous, uncouth, and devoid of all manners." The correct answer is BOORISH (Word 64).

7.   A

The question asks you to find a word that means a bitter denunciation. The correct answer is DIATRIBE (Word 100).

8.   C

The question asks you to find a word that means vague and lacking a detailed analysis. The correct answer is NEBULOUS (Word 59).

9.   E

The question asks you to find a word that would cause an "intense debate" and spark "partisanship." The correct answer is DIVISIVE (Word 91).

10.   D

The question asks you to find a word that means to be calm and composed under stressful conditions. The correct answer is EQUANIMITY (Word 80).

Chapter 3

YOU MEET THE MOST INTERESTING PEOPLE ON THE SAT: 101–130

History is filled with a fascinating array of men and women who have both made enduring contributions and caused great tragedies. This chapter will introduce you to 30 SAT words that describe an astonishing variety of people. For example, you will meet Pharaoh Akhenaton, the ancient world's most famous ICONOCLAST, and Bill Gates, the modern world's most generous PHILANTHROPIST. As you study this chapter, you will learn words that will help you describe great orators, notorious traitors, and astute political commentators. That's why we are convinced that you meet the most interesting people on the SAT!

101. CHARLATAN:
A fake; fraud; imposter; cheat

Would you trust the Wizard of Oz, Gilderoy Lockhart (*Harry Potter and the Chamber of Secrets*), or Frank Abagnale Jr. (*Catch Me If You Can*)? I hope not. All three of these men were CHARLATANS or imposters who could not be trusted. The Wizard of Oz was a CHARLATAN who tried to trick Dorothy and her friends. Gilderoy Lockhart was a CHARLATAN who interviewed famous wizards and witches and then took credit for their heroic deeds. And Frank Abagnale Jr. was a CHARLATAN who pretended to be an airline pilot and a surgeon.

 Tip for a Direct Hit

The word CHARLATAN often appears in sentence completion questions. It is important to remember that a CHARLATAN is associated with negative traits. A CHARLATAN will try to DUPE (mislead), UNWARY (incautious) victims with SPURIOUS (false) information.

102. SKEPTIC:
A person who doubts; a skeptic asks questions and lacks faith

In the movie *Men in Black*, Edwards was originally a SKEPTIC who did not believe that aliens were actually living in New York City. In *Bruce Almighty*, Bruce was originally a SKEPTIC who did not believe that the man he met was really God. And in the movie

Superbad, Seth was originally a SKEPTIC who did not believe Fogell's fake ID, with the name "McLovin" from Hawaii, would work.

103. RHETORICIAN:
An eloquent writer or speaker; a master of RHETORIC (the art of speaking and writing)

Frederick Douglass, Franklin Roosevelt, Martin Luther King Jr., John F. Kennedy, and Ronald Reagan were all CHARISMATIC (magnetic and inspiring) leaders and superb RHETORICIANS whose eloquent speeches inspired millions of people. For example, in his inaugural address, President Kennedy challenged Americans by proclaiming, "And so, my fellow Americans: ask not what your country can do for you – ask what you can do for your country."

104. HEDONIST:
A person who believes that pleasure is the chief goal of life

In Ancient Greece, the HEDONISTS urged their followers to "eat, drink, and be merry, for tomorrow we die." Although it is a long way from Ancient Greece to the home of rapper Ricky Ross in Miami, the HEDONISTIC principle of pursuing pleasure remains the same. During the tour of his "crib," Ross proudly displayed the interior of his Escalade Maybach, a Cadillac Escalade with the interior of a Maybach. Hooked up with leather seats, plasmas, and satellites, the interior provides everything a HEDONIST could possibly ask for and more.

105. ASCETIC:
A person who gives up material comforts and leads a life of self-denial, especially as an act of religious devotion

At the age of 29, Prince Siddhartha Gautama left the luxuries of his father's palace and for the next six years adopted an extreme ASCETIC life. For days at a time, he ate only a single grain of rice. His stomach became so empty that, by poking a finger into it, he could touch his backbone. Yet, Gautama gained only pain, not wisdom. He decided to give up extreme ASCETICISM and seek wisdom in other ways. Gautama was successful and soon became known as Buddha, a title meaning "the Enlightened One."

106. RACONTEUR:
A person who excels in telling ANECDOTES

Herodotus was an ancient Greek historian who was a renowned RACONTEUR. Many of the ANECDOTES (Word 213) in the movie *300* are taken from his famous history of the Persian Wars. For example, Herodotus recounts how a Persian officer tried to intimidate the Spartans by declaring that "A thousand nations of the Persian Empire descend upon you. Our arrows will blot out the sun." UNDAUNTED (Word 73), the Spartan warrior Stelios retorted, "Then we will fight in the shade."

107. ICONOCLAST:
A person who attacks and ridicules cherished figures, ideas, and institutions

What do the Egyptian pharaoh Akhenaton and the modern filmmaker Michael Moore have in common?

Both are ICONOCLASTS. Akhenaton challenged ancient Egypt's longstanding belief in a large number of gods by rejecting polytheism and insisting that Aton was the universal or only god. Michael Moore is a modern ICONOCLAST whose documentary films have attacked the Iraq War, the American health care system, Wall Street bankers, and Washington politicians. Like a true ICONOCLAST, Moore ridiculed Congress, saying that most of its members are scoundrels who deserve to be "removed and replaced."

108. DILETTANTE: dilettante

An amateur or dabbler; a person with a
SUPERFICIAL (Word 90) interest in an art or
a branch of knowledge

In the movie "Iron Man," Tony Stark enjoys being a DILETTANTE playboy who lets Obadiah Stane take care of the day-to-day operations of Stark Industries. However, behind his façade of being a DILETTANTE playboy, Tony is in reality a POLYMATH (a person of great and varied learning) who is a master engineer and inventor. Held prisoner by a terrorist group, Tony battles his way out of captivity by building a PROTOTYPE (Word 34) armored suit.

109. PARTISAN:

A person with strong and therefore biased
beliefs

Are you pro-life or pro-choice? Do you favor staying the course in Afghanistan or withdrawing the troops? Do you think bailing out the big Wall Street banks was a good or a bad policy? If you have a strong view on these issues, you are a PARTISAN. Remember, a PARTISAN speaks up and welcomes controversy. In contrast, NONPARTISAN issues enjoy widespread public support. For example, during the Cold War, most Americans supported the policy of containing Soviet expansion.

110. MENTOR:
An advisor; teacher; guide

ACOLYTE:
A devoted follower

In the Star Wars SAGA (Word 208), Obi-Wan Kenobi is a Jedi Knight who served as Luke Skywalker's MENTOR. As an eager young ACOLYTE, Skywalker learned the ways of the Force, a natural power harnessed by the Jedi in their struggle against the VILLAINOUS (vile, wicked) Darth Vader and evil Galactic Empire.

111. DEMAGOGUE:
A leader who appeals to the fears, emotions, and prejudices of the populace

Adolf Hitler is often cited as the epitome of a DEMA-GOGUE. Hitler rose to power by using impassioned speeches that appealed to the ethnic and nationalistic prejudices of the German people. Hitler exploited, embittered, and misled war veterans by blaming their plight on minorities and other convenient scapegoats.

Unfortunately, Americans have not been immune to the impassioned pleas of DEMAGOGUES. During the 1950s, Senator Joseph McCarthy falsely alleged that Communist sympathizers had infiltrated the State

Department. As McCarthy's DEMAGOGIC rhetoric grew bolder, he DENOUNCED (Word 176) General George Marshall, former Army Chief of Staff and ex-Secretary of State, as "part of a conspiracy so immense and an infamy so black as to dwarf any previous venture in the history of man."

112. AUTOMATON:

A self-operating machine; a mindless follower; a person who acts in a mechanical fashion

In the Harry Potter series, the Imperius Curse was a spell that caused its victim to fall under the command of the caster. In *Harry Potter and the Deathly Hallows*, the Death Eater Yaxley placed an Imperius Curse on Pius Thickness. When Thickness became Minister of Magic, he behaved like an AUTOMATON or mindless follower of Lord Voldemort.

113. RECLUSE:

A person who leads a secluded or solitary life

What do Harper Lee, Sybill Trelawney, and Greta Garbo have in common? All three were RECLUSES who wanted to live alone. Although she is the world-famous author of *To Kill a Mockingbird*, Harper Lee rarely appears in public. Sybill Trelawney was the Divination professor at Hogwarts who lived alone in the North Tower because she didn't want to "cloud her Inner Eye." And Greta Garbo was a famous actress who summed up what it means to be a RECLUSE when she said: "I want to be alone."

114. BUNGLER:

Someone who is clumsy or INEPT; a person who makes mistakes because of incompetence

BUNGLERS have been featured in a number of movies and television programs. For example, *The Three Stooges* were a trio of BUNGLERS whose INEPT blunders and madcap antics never failed to leave their fans laughing. In the movie *Mighty Ducks*, the team was a group of BUNGLERS that did not know how to play hockey or work together. One of television's most beloved BUNGLERS was Gilligan, the clumsy first mate on *Gilligan's Island*.

115. CLAIRVOYANT:

Having the supposed power to see objects and events that cannot be perceived with the five traditional senses; a SEER

Sybill Trelawney was the Divination professor at Hogwarts who claimed to be a CLAIRVOYANT. She used tea leaves and crystal balls to see the future. Both Harry and Professor Dumbledore were SKEPTICAL (Word 102) about her claim to be a CLAIRVOYANT. In *Harry Potter and the Order of the Phoenix*, Dolores Umbridge fired Sybill for being a CHARLATAN (Word 101). Nonetheless, readers of the Harry Potter series know that Trelawney did make two extremely important and very accurate prophecies.

116. PROGNOSTICATOR:

A person who makes predictions based upon current information and data

Weather forecasters, sports announcers, and financial analysts are all PROGNOSTICATORS who use information and data to make predictions and forecasts. It is important to understand the difference between a PROGNOSTICATOR and a CLAIRVOYANT (Word 115). Although both make predictions, a PROGNOSTICAT-OR uses empirical data that can be collected, seen, and studied. In contrast, a CLAIRVOYANT claims to see the future through means beyond the five senses.

117. PUNDIT:
An expert commentator; an authority who expresses his or her opinion, usually on political issues

From CNN's News Center to ESPN's Sports Center, television programs are filled with PUNDITS who offer their "expert" commentary on issues ranging from political campaigns to March Madness brackets. The PUNDITS almost always sound authoritative and convincing. But it is wise to maintain a healthy SKEPTICISM (Word 102). Here are expert opinions from famous pundits that turned out to be wrong:

> *"Louis Pasteur's theory of germs is ridiculous fiction."*
>> Pierre Packet, Professor of Physiology at Toulouse, 1872

> *"Heavier-than-air flying machines are impossible."*
>> Lord Kelvin, President of the Royal Society, 1895

> *"Stocks have reached what looks like a permanently high plateau."*
>> Irving Fisher, Professor of Economics, Yale University, 1929

"There is no reason anyone would want a computer in their home."

> Ken Olson, President, Chairman, and Founder of Digital Equipment Corp., 1977

118. ZEALOT:

A very enthusiastic person; a champion; a true believer

William Lloyd Garrison was a ZEALOT who championed the cause of unconditional and immediate abolition. In the first issue of *The Liberator*, Garrison left no doubt as to his intentions when he wrote: "I am in earnest – I will not equivocate – I will not excuse – I will not retreat a single inch – AND I WILL BE HEARD."

119. NEOPHYTE, NOVICE, GREENHORN:

All three are beginners

In October 2008, Justin Bieber was an unknown NEOPHYTE who had never professionally recorded a song. However, Usher recognized that although Bieber was NOVICE, he was a musical PRODIGY (Word 123) who had the potential to become a superstar. With Usher as his MENTOR (Word 110), the angelic-looking Bieber soon developed a "street-wise" look that included baseball caps, hoodies, hip hop chains, and flashy sneakers. Usher quickly transformed Bieber from a GREENHORN to a global sensation. In July 2010, JB's music video *Baby* SUPPLANTED (replaced) Lady Gaga's *Bad Romance* video as the most viewed YouTube video ever.

120. BENEFACTOR and PATRON:
A person who makes a gift or bequest

BENEFICIARY:
The recipient of funds, titles, property, and other benefits

Nicholas Sparks has achieved international fame by writing romance novels such as *The Notebook* and *A Walk to Remember* that are often set in New Bern, North Carolina. Residents of New Bern also know Sparks as a generous BENEFACTOR and PATRON who has donated nearly $1 million dollars to build a state-of-the-art track and field facility for New Bern High School. As the BENEFICIARIES of this MUNIFICENT (Word 232) gift, the New Bern Bears have become one of North Carolina's top track and field teams. Note that both BENEFACTOR and BENEFICIARY begin with the Latin prefix *bene*, which means "good." So a BENEFACTOR, like Nicholas Sparks, gives good gifts, and a BENEFICIARY, like New Bern High School, receives good gifts.

121. DISSEMBLER and PREVARICATOR:
Both are liars and deceivers

In *Mean Girls*, Regina George was a cunning DISSEMBLER who deliberately lied to her friends and to her enemies. In the movie *Pirates of the Caribbean: Curse of the Black Pearl*, Captain Barbarossa was a PREVARICATOR who repeatedly lied to Jack Sparrow, Elizabeth Swann, and Will Turner.

122. PROPONENT:

One who argues in support of something; an ADVOCATE; a champion of a cause

Although America has faced a number of challenging social problems, our nation has always produced leaders who were strong PROPONENTS of reform. For example, during the 19th century, Jane Addams was an outspoken PROPONENT for urban settlement houses. Today, former Vice-President Al Gore is a vigorous ADVOCATE of implementing measures that will reduce global warming. One way to remember PROPONENT is to note that the prefix *pro* means to be for something.

123. PRODIGY:

A person with great talent; a young genius

What do Wolfgang Mozart and Pablo Picasso have in common? Both were PRODIGIES who demonstrated uncanny artistic talent at a young age. Mozart was a child PRODIGY who wrote his first symphony at the age of eight and grew into a PROLIFIC (Word 347) adult who wrote over 600 pieces of music before dying at the age of 35. Like Mozart, Picasso demonstrated PRECOCIOUS (very advanced) talent by drawing pictures before he could talk. Picasso mastered many styles but is best known as the PROGENITOR (originator) of Cubism.

124. ORACLE:

A person considered to be a source of wise counsel or prophetic opinions

Would you like to know what is going to happen in the future? All you have to do is ask an ORACLE. While the ancient Greeks asked the Delphic Oracle to predict the future, World Cup soccer fans watched televised reports featuring the predictions of an octopus named Paul. The eight-legged ORACLE became a global sensation when he correctly predicted the winner of eight straight matches. Paul's PROGNOSTICATIONS (Word 116) have attracted LUCRATIVE (Word 227) offers from people who want to know the outcome of elections and the gender of future children.

125. MISANTHROPE:
A person who hates or distrusts humankind

Ebenezer Scrooge and Alceste are two of the best known MISANTHROPES in literature. Scrooge is the main character in Charles Dickens's 1843 novel, *A Christmas Carol*. He is a cold-hearted, MISERLY (very stingy) MISANTHROPE who despises poor people and Christmas. Alceste is the main character in Molière's 1666 play, *Misanthrope*. He is a judgmental MISANTHROPE, quick to criticize the flaws in people.

 Tip for a Direct Hit

MISANTHROPE combines the Greek prefix *miso* meaning "hate" with the Greek root *anthropos* meaning "humankind." Prefixes make a difference in the meaning of words. If we place the Greek prefix *philo*, meaning "love," in front of *anthropos*, we will have the word PHILANTHROPY, meaning love of humankind. A PHILANTHROPIST loves humanity so much that he or she donates time and money to charity.

126. INNOVATOR:
A person who introduces something new

What do D.W. Griffith and James Cameron have in common? Both are cinematic INNOVATORS whose pioneering works have had a profound impact on movies. Griffith's groundbreaking film *The Birth of a Nation* (1915) included such SEMINAL (highly influential and original) camera techniques as jump-cuts and facial close-ups. Running an UNPRECEDENTED (Word 259) 3 hours and 10 minutes, *The Birth of a Nation* ushered in a new era of blockbuster films.

Like D. W. Griffith, James Cameron is recognized as an INNOVATOR whose work is redefining the art of special effects. *Avatar* (2009) is a visually stunning movie that uses a 3D Fusion Camera System to seamlessly sew human actors into a digital world in real time.

127. SYCOPHANT:
A person who seeks favor by flattering people of influence; a TOADY; someone who behaves in an OBSEQUIOUS or servile manner

Louis XIV compelled France's great nobles to live at the Versailles Palace. Life at the royal palace transformed HAUGHTY (arrogant) aristocrats into favor-seeking SYCOPHANTS. Instead of competing for political power, nobles SQUANDERED (wasted) their fortunes jockeying for social prestige. For example, nobles vied for the COVETED (Word 32) honor of holding Louis XIV's shirt as he prepared to get dressed.

128. STOIC:

A person who is seemingly INDIFFERENT (Word 10) to or unaffected by joy, grief, pleasure, or pain; someone who is impassive and emotionless

What would you do if you scored the winning goal in a championship soccer game? What would you do if your error caused your team to lose a championship baseball game? Most people would be elated to win and dejected to lose. However, a STOIC would remain impassive, showing no emotion in victory or defeat.

Being a STOIC is not easy. It requires great discipline and self-control. For example, tourists to London are familiar with the distinctive bearskin helmets and scarlet uniforms worn by the guards at Buckingham Palace. The guards are famous for their ability to STOICALLY endure hot summer weather and hordes of pesky tourists.

129. REPROBATE:

A morally unprincipled person

Who is the most despised REPROBATE living in America today? For thousands of betrayed investors there is only one answer – Bernard Madoff. On June 29, 2009, Judge Denny Chin sentenced Madoff to 150 years in prison for running a giant Ponzi scheme that cheated investors out of almost 65 billion dollars. Madoff's victims included pension funds, charitable institutions, and elderly retirees. Although Madoff was a CHARLATAN (Word 101), he is best described as a REPROBATE because of the enormity of a fraud that Judge Chin called "extraordinarily evil."

130. RENEGADE:

A disloyal person who betrays his or her cause; a traitor; a deserter

In 1777, Benedict Arnold was one of America's most admired Revolutionary War generals. Yet, just three years later, Arnold was vilified as a RENEGADE whose name became synonymous with traitor. What happened to cause this amazing change in Arnold's reputation? Despite his bravery at the pivotal battle of Saratoga, Arnold was passed over for promotion while other officers took credit for his accomplishments. Frustrated and bitter, Arnold secretly became a British agent. In 1780, he obtained command of West Point in order to surrender it to the British. American forces discovered Arnold's treacherous scheme, and he was forced to flee to London to avoid capture. Today, Arnold's contributions to the colonial cause are forgotten, and he is remembered as our nation's first and foremost RENEGADE.

 Tip for a Direct Hit

The words REPROBATE (Word 129) and RENEGADE (Word 130) are easy to confuse. They sound similar and both are negative words used to describe despicable people. Nonetheless, there are important differences between the people described by these two words. A REPROBATE is best remembered as a morally unprincipled and evil person. A RENEGADE is best remembered as a traitor and deserter.

Testing Your Vocabulary

Each SAT contains 19 sentence completion questions that are primarily a test of your vocabulary. Each sentence completion will always have a key word or phrase that will lead you to the correct answer. Use the vocabulary from Chapters 1-3 to circle the answer to each of the following 10 sentence completion questions. You'll find answers and explanations on pages 85 to 87.

1.   Like a true _____, Drew had a number of constantly shifting interests and hobbies.

    (A) dilettante
    (B) hedonist
    (C) ascetic
    (D) philanthropist
    (E) dissembler

2.   Belgian artist James Ensor was often called _____ because he preferred to live and work alone in the attic of his parent's home in Ostend.

    (A) a charlatan
    (B) an automaton
    (C) an iconoclast
    (D) a recluse
    (E) a skeptic

3.   Critics accused the used car salesman of being a
     _____ because he tried to dupe customers with
     fraudulent information.

     (A) novice
     (B) charlatan
     (C) prodigy
     (D) sycophant
     (E) clairvoyant

4.   Much of Frederick Douglass' prestige and
     influence came from his skill with the spoken
     word; he was a great _____ at a time when
     eloquent oratory was widely _____.

     (A) raconteur .. disparaged
     (B) pundit .. spurned
     (C) rhetorician .. valued
     (D) mediator .. ignored
     (E) prognosticator .. denounced

5.   Because Benedict Arnold switched his allegiance
     to the British, patriots branded him a _____,
     and even his new allies justifiably considered
     him an opportunist.

     (A) bungler
     (B) hedonist
     (C) renegade
     (D) demagogue
     (E) oracle

6. As a habitual skeptic, Jordan has always been
   _____ to _____ what others believe to be
   conventional wisdom.

   (A) prone .. misinterpret
   (B) eager .. substantiate
   (C) content .. acknowledge
   (D) reluctant .. doubt
   (E) inclined .. question

7. The _____ prediction was astonishingly
   _____: it offered a bold view of the future that
   no one had foreseen.

   (A) prognosticator's .. unconventional
   (B) partisan's .. obvious
   (C) iconoclast's .. orthodox
   (D) pundit's .. fleeting
   (E) demagogue's prudent

8. The coach was a(n) _____ by nature: she
   remained impassive when her team won and
   _____ when they lost.

   (A) hedonist .. morose
   (B) zealot .. anguished
   (C) stoic .. emotionless
   (D) iconoclast .. genial
   (E) raconteur .. affable

9. As _____, Ashley delighted in disputing
   sacrosanct beliefs, questioning established
   authorities, and challenging long-held practices.

   (A) a mediator
   (B) a sycophant
   (C) a mentor
   (D) an iconoclast
   (E) a beneficiary

10. Although Brandon claimed to be neutral, he was clearly a _____ who had strong and biased views on the key issues under consideration.

    (A) partisan
    (B) dilettante
    (C) rhetorician
    (D) skeptic
    (E) bungler

Answers and Explanations

1. A

The question asks you to find a word describing a person who has "constantly shifting interests and hobbies." The correct answer is DILET-TANTE (Word 108) because a DILETTANTE is a dabbler who has shifting interests.

2. D

The question asks you to find a word describing a person who "preferred to live and work alone." The correct answer is RECLUSE (Word 113) because a RECLUSE prefers to live a secluded solitary life.

3. B

The question asks you to find a word describing a person who "tried to dupe customers with fraudulent information." The correct answer is CHARLATAN (Word 101) because a CHARLATAN is a fake or fraud who tries to dupe and cheat unsuspecting people.

4. C

The question asks you to find a first word describing Frederick Douglass. You are told that he was an "eloquent" orator who had great "skill with the spoken word." The second work must be positive because Douglass derived great "prestige and influence" from his oratory. The correct answer is RHETORICIAN (Word 103) and VALUED, because a RHETORICIAN is an eloquent speaker and VALUED is a positive second word. Note that answer A is tempting because a RACONTEUR is a great storyteller. However, DISPARAGED (Word 93) is a negative word meaning to belittle or slight.

5. **C**

The question asks you to find a word describing a person who "switched his allegiance." The correct answer is RENEGADE (Word 130) because a RENEGADE is a traitor or disloyal person.

6. **E**

The question asks you to find a pair of answers that describe how a "habitual skeptic" would behave. The correct answer is SKEPTIC (Word 102) because a SKEPTIC is a doubter who is inclined to question "conventional beliefs."

7. **A**

The question asks you to find a first word describing a person who makes predictions and a second word describing those predictions as both "bold" and so farsighted that they had not been "foreseen." The correct answer is PROGNOSTICATOR (Word 116) and UNCON-VENTIOANAL (Word 7) because a PROG-NOSTICATOR makes predictions and these predictions would be UNCONVENTIONAL because they are both "bold" and unforeseen.

8. **C**

The question asks you to find a first word describing a coach who is impassive when her team wins and a second word that is consistent with both the first word and impassive. The correct answer is STOIC (Word 128) and EMOTIONLESS because a STOIC is "impassive" and emotionless in both victory and defeat.

9.   D

The question asks you to find a person who delights in "disputing sacrosanct beliefs, questioning established authorities, and challenging long-held practices." The correct answer is ICONOCLAST (Word 107) because an ICONOCLAST attacks cherished ideas and institutions.

10.   A

The question asks you to find a person who claimed to be neutral but in reality has "strong and biased views." The correct answer is PARTISAN (WORD 109) because a PARTISAN is a person with strongly-held and therefore biased views.

Chapter 4

EVERY SAT WORD HAS A HISTORY: 131–155

In 1922, British archaeologist Howard Carter amazed the world by discovering Pharaoh Tutankhamen's tomb. Each of the dazzling artifacts that he unearthed yielded new insights into Egyptian history.

Although we usually don't think of them in this way, words are like historic artifacts. Like the precious jewels Carter found, words also have fascinating histories. ETYMOLOGY is a branch of linguistics that specializes in digging up the origins of words.

Each word in our language has a unique history. The English language contains an especially rich collection of words derived from legends, places, customs, and names. These "history-based" words are frequently tested on the SAT.

Our etymological tour will begin in ancient Greece and Rome. We will then explore words from the Middle Ages, European history and literature, and American folklore and politics. Our tour will conclude with words from India and the work of Arab astronomers.

A.   ANCIENT GREECE

131. DRACONIAN:
Characterized by very strict laws, rules, and punishments

Draco was an ancient Athenian ruler who believed that the city-state's haphazard judicial system needed to be reformed. In 621 B.C.E., he issued a comprehensive but very severe new code of laws. Whether trivial or serious, most criminal offenses called for the death penalty. Draco's laws were so severe that they were said to be written not in ink but in blood.

Today, the word DRACONIAN refers to very strict laws, rules, and punishments. For example, in Iran both men and women can be stoned to death as punishment for being convicted of adultery.

132. LACONIC:
Very brief; concise; SUCCINCT; TERSE

The ancient city-state of Sparta was located in a region of Greece called Laconia. The Spartans were fearless warriors who had little time for long speeches. As a result, they were renowned for being LACONIC or very concise. For example, Philip of Macedon, father of Alexander the Great, sent the Spartans a long list of demands. The LACONIC Spartans sent it back with a one word answer: "No!"

Today, the word LACONIC still means very brief, TERSE. In the movie *The Bourne Ultimatum*, for example, Jason Bourne is very SUCCINCT. Here is a TERSE dialogue between Bourne and Marie's brother:

Marie's Brother: Where's my sister?

Jason Bourne: Why don't you sit down?

Marie's Brother: Where is she?

Jason Bourne: She was killed. I'm sorry.

Marie's Brother: How did she die?

Jason Bourne: She was shot. We were together in India. He came for me.

Marie's Brother: Did you kill him?

Jason Bourne: Yes.

133. SPARTAN:
Plain; simple; AUSTERE (Word 19)

The Spartans were more than just LACONIC. They also prided themselves on being tough warriors who avoided luxuries and led hardy lives. For example, Spartan soldiers lived in army barracks and ate meager servings of a coarse black porridge.

Today, the word SPARTAN still describes a plain life without luxuries. Like the ancient Spartans, American soldiers undergo a rigorous period of training. For example, recruits at the Marine training center at Paris Island must live in SPARTAN barracks and pass an ARDUOUS (demanding) twelve-week training schedule before they can be called United States Marines.

134. HALCYON:
Idyllically calm and peaceful; an untroubled golden time of happiness and tranquility

In Greek mythology, Alcyone was the daughter of Aeolus, god of the winds, and the devoted wife of Ceyx. When Ceyx tragically drowned in a shipwreck, the distraught Alcyone threw herself into the sea. Out of compassion, the gods transformed Alcyone and Ceyx into a pair of kingfishers. The ancient Greeks named this distinctive bird *halkyon* after Alcyone. According to legend, kingfishers built a floating nest on the sea at about the time of the winter solstice in December. To protect their nest, the gods ordered the winds to remain calm for a week before and after the winter solstice. The expression "halcyon days" refers to this period of untroubled peace and tranquility.

Today, HALCYON still refers to a golden time of untroubled happiness and tranquility. In the movie, *The Notebook*, Allie and Noah are two carefree teenagers who meet at a local carnival in Seabrook, North Carolina. Although they are from very different backgrounds, the two teenagers are instantly smitten with each other and spend a romantic summer together. These HALCYON days inspired their lifelong love for each other.

135. SOPHISTRY:
A plausible but deliberately misleading or FALLACIOUS argument designed to deceive someone

The Sophists were originally a respected group of ancient Greek philosophers who specialized in teaching rhetoric. However, over time they gained a reputation for their ability to persuade by using clever and often misleading arguments. Today, SOPHISTRY is a negative word that refers to a PLAUSIBLE (Word 38) but deliberately misleading argument.

In the movie *Animal House*, the Deltas are a notorious group of fun-loving misfits who gleefully break campus rules. Outraged by their low grades and wild parties, Dean Wormer holds a hearing to revoke the Deltas' charter. UNDAUNTED (Word 73) by Dean Wormer's accusations, Otter resorts to SOPHISTRY in a clever but FUTILE (Word 46) attempt to save the Deltas:

> *"Ladies and gentlemen, I'll be brief. The issue here is not whether we broke a few rules or took a few liberties with our female party guests – we did. But you can't hold a whole fraternity responsible for the behavior of few sick, twisted individuals. For if you do, then shouldn't we blame the whole fraternity system? And if the whole fraternity system is guilty, then isn't this an indictment of our educational institutions in general? I put it to you – isn't this an indictment of our entire American society? Well, you can do whatever you want to us, but we're not going to sit here and listen to you badmouth the United States of America. Gentlemen!"*

Pleased with his SOPHISTRY, Otter then leads the defiant Deltas out of the chamber as all the fraternity brothers hum the Star-Spangled Banner.

136. CHIMERICAL:
Given to fantastic schemes; existing only as a product of an unchecked imagination

The *Chimera* was one of the most fearsome monsters in Greek mythology. A fire-breathing female, it had the head and body of a lion, a serpent's tail, and a goat's head protruding from its midsection. This frightening combination was unusually fantastic even for the ancient Greeks. The creature's element of unchecked imagination survives in the word CHIMERICAL.

Today, a CHIMERICAL scheme or claim is one that is a product of unrestrained fantasy. For example, according to popular legend, Ponce de Leon discovered Florida while searching for the fabled Fountain of Youth. While the Fountain of Youth proved to be fanciful, we have still not given up our search for longevity. Fad diets, vitamin supplements, and exercise routines all offer claims that have often proved to be CHIMERICAL.

 Tip for a Direct Hit

CHIMERICAL is a difficult word that often appears in challenging sentence completion questions. Typically, test writers associate CHIMERICAL with once-promising medical advances that were never fully realized and were thus CHIMERICAL.

137. OSTRACIZE:
To deliberately exclude from a group

In ancient Athens, an *ostrakon* was a broken fragment or shard from an earthen vessel. The Athenians used these pot shards as ballots in an annual vote to decide who, if anyone, should be banished from their city. Each voter wrote a name on his *ostrakon*. If at least 6,000 votes were cast and if a majority of them named one man, then that man was banished or OSTRACIZED and had to leave Athens for a year.

Today, the word OSTRACIZE still retains its original meaning of deliberately excluding someone from a group. For example, following World War II, angry French citizens OSTRACIZED people who had collaborated with the Nazis. In Chartres, vigilantes shaved the head of a young woman whose baby was fathered by a German soldier. Crowds of jeering people taunted the OSTRACIZED woman as she walked alone on the city streets.

B. ANCIENT ROME

138. IMPECUNIOUS:
Poor; penniless; NOT AFFLUENT(Word 231)

When the Romans first settled the lands along the Tiber River, they lacked a metal currency. Nonetheless, Roman farmers did have an ample supply of cattle. As a result, cattle were often used as a measure of wealth. In Latin, *pecus* is the word for cattle. A Roman without a cow or *pecus* was thus IMPECUNIOUS (IM is a prefix meaning NOT) or NOT WEALTHY.

Today, the word IMPECUNIOUS means lacking money and, thus, poor. In the movie *Titanic*, Rose fell in love with a handsome but IMPECUNIOUS young artist named Jack Dawson. In the movie *Knocked Up*, Ben Stone is an IMPECUNIOUS slacker who has no job and no money. He eats a lot of spaghetti and doesn't own a phone because of "payment complications." Ben has been living for years off a $14,000 settlement check he received after a postal truck ran over his foot. He only has about $900 left.

139. NEFARIOUS:
Extremely wicked; villainous; vile

In ancient Rome, the Latin word *nefarius* referred to a criminal. This unsavory connotation continued over the centuries. Today, the word NEFARIOUS is used to describe someone who is extremely wicked. Lord Voldemort (*Harry Potter*), the Joker (*The Dark Knight*), and Darth Vader (*Star Wars*) form a PANTHEON (group of noted individuals) of cinema's most NEFARIOUS villains.

140. JOVIAL:
Good-humored; cheerful; JOCULAR

Jupiter was the chief deity of the Roman Empire. The Romans believed that each of their gods possessed particular attributes of character. As the most powerful god, Jupiter was both majestic and authoritative. However, he was also believed to be fun-loving and the source of joy and happiness. Since Jupiter was also known as Jove, the word JOVIAL came to refer to people who have a cheerful, jolly temperament.

Today, JOVIAL still retains its meaning of good-humored, cheerful, and JOCULAR. While most people do not associate JOVIAL with Jupiter, they do associate the word with Santa Claus. Often referred to as "JOVIAL old St. Nicholas," Santa Claus is usually presented as a jolly, good-humored man who brings presents to well-behaved children.

C. MIDDLE AGES

141. DIRGE:
A funeral hymn; a slow mournful musical composition

When medieval Christians gathered to pay their final respects to the deceased, the Church ceremony began with this solemn Latin phrase:

"Dirige, Domine, Deus meus, in conspectus tuo viam meam."
("Direct, O Lord my God, my way in thy sight.")

Today, a DIRGE refers to a sad, mournful song or hymn of lament. For example, as the Titanic slowly sank, its musicians played the DIRGE "Nearer, My God, To Thee" to comfort the desperate souls still on the doomed ship. As POIGNANTLY (Word 77) depicted in the movie, the band played the slow, mournful DIRGE until the very end. They then calmly went down with their ship.

142. MAUDLIN:
Tearful; excessively sentimental

Mary Magdalene played an important and recurring role in the Gospel accounts of Christ's life and death.

According to the Gospels, she stood at the foot of the cross, saw Christ laid in the tomb, and was the first recorded witness of the Resurrection. During the 15th century, artists frequently portrayed Mary Magdalene weeping as Christ was being taken down from the Cross. The word MAUDLIN is an alteration of the name Magdalene. Today MAUDLIN refers to excessively sentimental behavior.

Fans of the Harry Potter novels will recall that Moaning Myrtle lives up to her name by crying incessantly and thus being MAUDLIN. And fans of *The Notebook* will recall that the movie contains many MAUDLIN scenes. For example, did you cry when Noah and Allie died in each other's arms?

D.   EUROPEAN HISTORY AND LITERATURE

143. QUIXOTIC:
Foolishly impractical in the pursuit of ideals; impractical idealism

Miguel de Cervantes' epic novel *Don Quixote* describes the chivalric adventures of the would-be knight Don Quixote. Motivated by chivalric ideals, Don Quixote is determined to undo the wrongs of the world. Blinded by his excited imagination, Don Quixote turns lonely inns into castles and windmills into fearsome giants. After a long series of misadventures, Don Quixote returns home a tired and disillusioned old man. Derived from his name, the modern word QUIXOTIC refers to the foolish and impractical pursuit of noble but unattainable ideals.

In the movie *Little Miss Sunshine*, the Hoovers are a dysfunctional family from Albuquerque, New Mexico. Their selfish concerns and petty squabbles are interrupted when seven-year-old Olive learns she has qualified to compete in the "Little Miss Sunshine" beauty pageant in Redondo Beach, California. Despite facing impending bankruptcy, the family departs on a QUIXOTIC journey to reach Redondo Beach and give Olive a chance to make her dream come true.

144. PANDEMONIUM:
A wild uproar; tumult

In Book I of *Paradise Lost*, the fallen Satan commands his heralds to proclaim, "A solemn Councel forthwith to be held/At Pandemonium, the high Capital/Of Satan and his Peers." John Milton COINED (Word 269) this name for the capital of Hell by combining the prefix pan, meaning "all," with the Late Latin word *daemonium*, meaning "evil spirit." As Satan's capital, Pandemonium was characterized by noise, confusion, and wild uproar.

Today, the word PANDEMONIUM refers to a wild uproar rather than to a specific place. The movie *I Am Legend* vividly portrays the PANDEMONIUM that gripped the residents of New York City as they desperately tried to flee the stricken city. While the PANDEMONIUM portrayed in *I Am Legend* was fictional, residents of New York City living in lower Manhattan experienced an all-too-real PANDEMONIUM as the Trade Towers collapsed on 9/11.

Tip for a Direct Hit

The prefix *pan* is in a number of words that are ALL around you. For example, a PANORAMIC view enables you to see in ALL directions. A PANACEA is a remedy that will supposedly cure ALL diseases. And finally, PANOPLY is a complete suit of armor and thus any covering that has ALL the necessary array of materials.

145. MARTINET:
A strict disciplinarian; a person who demands absolute adherence to forms and rules

The French king Louis XIV dreamed of winning glory by expanding France's boundaries to the Rhine River and the Alps. To achieve this goal, Louis and his war minister, the Marquis de Louvois, created Europe's first professional army. In order to be effective, the new army required strict discipline. Louvois assigned this exacting task to Colonel Jean Martinet. A stern drillmaster, Martinet trained his troops to march in linear formations at exactly 80 paces a minute. The rigid control imposed by Martinet helped transform NOVICE (Word 119) soldiers into highly-disciplined fighting units.

Today, the word MARTINET still refers to a strict disciplinarian. The Marine Drill Sergeants at Paris Island are renowned for being merciless MARTINETS. As readers of Harry Potter are well aware, MARTINETS are not limited to the military. In *Harry Potter and the Order of the Phoenix*, Dolores Umbridge was a MARTINET who tried to impose rigid standards of discipline on the students and faculty at Hogwarts.

146. FIASCO:
A complete failure; a DEBACLE

Venetian glassblowers were renowned for their skill in making intricate glass vases and bowls. Italian etymologists theorize that when a master craftsman discovered a flaw in a piece he was working on, he would turn it into an ordinary bottle to avoid wasting the glass. Since *"far fiasco"* is an Italian phrase meaning "to make a bottle," the bottle would represent a failure and thus a FIASCO.

Today, the word FIASCO still refers to a complete failure or DEBACLE. Most observers believe that the government's and BP's BELATED (tardy, slow) response to the Gulf Oil Spill transformed a disaster into a devastating human-made DEBACLE.

147. BOWDLERIZE:
To remove or delete parts of a book, song or other work that are considered offensive

Would you read a story or play containing profanity and sexual references? Probably not. For example, wouldn't you be tempted to substitute "jerk" and "butt" for some less printable words? Dr. Thomas Bowdler, an English physician, thought parents should read Shakespeare's plays to their children. Although Shakespeare may be an immortal bard, his plays do contain profanity and suggestive scenes that may not be appropriate for family reading. So in 1818, Bowdler decided to publish a family edition of Shakespeare. In his preface, Bowdler noted that he carefully edited "those words and expressions which cannot, with propriety, be read aloud to a family." Outraged critics attacked Bowdler and COINED (Word 269) the new word BOWDLERIZE to describe the deletion of parts of a book or play that are deemed offensive. It is interesting to note that the BOWDLERIZED edition of Shakespeare proved to be a commercial success, thus vindicating Bowdler's judgment.

The controversy over BOWDLERIZED books did not end with Thomas Bowdler. In her book *The Language Police*, Diane Ravitch argues that American students are compelled to read bland texts that have been BOWDLERIZED by publishers and textbook committees who willingly cut controversial material from their books. For example, an anthology used in Tennessee schools changed "By God!" to "By gum!", and California rejected a reading book because *The Little Engine That Could* was male.

148. GALVANIZE:
To electrify; to stir into action as if with an electric shock

Luigi Galvani (1737–1790) was an Italian professor of physiology whose pioneering work stimulated important research into the nature of electricity. Galvani's name is still associated with electricity.

Today, the word GALVANIZE means to electrify, to stir into action as if with an electric shock. Rosa Park's simple but powerful act of protest GALVANIZED the

Montgomery Bus Boycott, thus giving additional IM-PETUS (Word 78) to the Civil Rights Movement.

E.   AMERICAN FOLKLORE AND POLITICS

149. PICAYUNE:
Something of small value or importance; petty; trifling

The *New Orleans Times-Picayune* has one of the best-known and oddest names of an American newspaper. The word "picayune" originally referred to a small Spanish coin worth about six cents. Back in 1837, the original proprietors of the then *New Orleans Picayune* gave their new paper that name because a copy cost about six cents, or one picayune.

Today, the word PICAYUNE refers to something of small value and thus of little importance. New Orleans leaders angrily accused FEMA officials of ignoring urgent problems while they focused on minor details that could best be described as PICAYUNE.

150. GERRYMANDER:
To divide a geographic area into voting districts so as to give unfair advantage to one party in elections

If you think the word GERRYMANDER sounds like the name of a strange political beast, you are right. The name was COINED (Word 269) by combining the word salamander, "a small lizard-like amphibian," with the last name of Elbridge Gerry, a former governor of Massachusetts. Gerry was immortalized in this word because an election district created by members of his party in 1812 looked like a salamander. When the famous artist Gilbert Stuart noticed the oddly-shaped district on a map in a newspaper editor's office, he decorated the outline of the district with a head, wings, and claws and then said to the editor, "That will do for a salamander!" "Gerrymander!" came the reply and a new SAT word was COINED or created.

Today, the word GERRYMANDER still retains its meaning of an oddly-shaped district designed to favor one party. For example, California drew district lines so that two pockets of Republican strength in Los Angeles separated by many miles were connected by a thin strip of coastline. In this way, most Republican voters were assigned to one GERRYMANDERED district.

151. MAVERICK:
An independent individual who does not go along with a group or party; a nonconformist

Samuel A. Maverick was one of the early leaders of Texas. He fought for Texas independence, served as mayor of San Antonio, and eventually purchased a 385,000 acre ranch. While Maverick's achievements have been forgotten, his name is remembered because of his practice of refusing to brand the cattle on his ranch. These unbranded cattle were soon called *mavericks*.

Today, the meaning of the word MAVERICK has been extended from cattle to people. A MAVERICK is anyone who doesn't follow the common herd. A MAVERICK is thus a nonconformist. For example, in the movie *Top Gun*, Lt. Peter Mitchell received the nickname "Mav" because he was a nonconformist who did not always follow the rules.

F. INDIA

152. JUGGERNAUT:
An irresistible force that crushes everything in its path

Jagannath (or "Lord of the World") is an incarnation of the Hindu god Vishnu. In the early 14th century, a Franciscan missionary named Friar Odoric visited India. When he returned to Europe, Odoric published a journal describing how Jagannath's devoted follow-ers placed the god's image on an enormous carriage which they pulled through the streets. According to Odoric's inaccurate but sensational report, excited worshippers threw themselves under the carriage and were crushed to death. As Odoric's exaggerated story spread across Europe, Jagannath's name was trans-formed into the new word JUGGERNAUT.

Today, the word JUGGERNAUT refers to an irresistible force that crushes everything in its path. The D-Day assault forces were a JUGGERNAUT that crushed the German defenses.

153. SERENDIPITY:
An accidental but fortunate discovery

Sri Lanka is an island off the southeast coast of India. Known to Arab geographers as Serendip, the exotic island was the setting of a fanciful Persian fairy tale, *The Three Princes of Serendip*. The story and its title inspired the English writer Horace Walpole (1717-1797) to COIN (Word 269) the word *serendipity*. In a letter written in 1754, Walpole explained that *serendipity* refers to the uncanny ability of the three princes to make chance discoveries.

Today, the word SERENDIPITY refers to an accidental but fortunate discovery. When Scottish physician Alexander Fleming went on vacation in 1928, he left a dish smeared with Staphylococcus bacteria on a bench in his laboratory. In his absence, a mold from another lab drifted onto the culture. When Fleming returned, he noticed that the bacteria had not grown where the mold had fallen. Fleming named the active ingredient in the mold penicillin. His SEREN-DIPITOUS discovery proved to be a WATERSHED (Word 242) event in modern medicine. Penicillin is still one of the most effective antibiotics used around the world.

G.   ARAB ASTRONOMY

154. ZENITH:
The highest point; the peak; APEX

Arab astronomers called the point of the celestial sphere directly above the observer the *samt*, meaning "way of the head." When Muslims conquered the Iberian Peninsula, many Arabic words entered the Spanish language. Within a short time, the Arabic word *samt* became the Spanish word *zenit*. Over time, *zenit* passed into English and became ZENITH.

Today, the word ZENITH refers to the highest point or peak. On June 12, 1987, President Ronald Reagan spoke for the people of West Berlin and the entire Free World when he called upon Soviet leader Mikhail Gorbachev to "tear down" the Berlin Wall. Reagan's dramatic speech marked the ZENITH of his presidency and the beginning of the end of the Cold War.

155. NADIR:
The lowest point; the bottom

Arab astronomers called the point of the celestial sphere directly under the observer the nazir, or opposite. Thus, the phrase *nazir as-samt* meant "opposite the zenith." With a slight modification, *nazir* entered the English language as NADIR.

Today, the word NADIR is used to describe someone's lowest point. The days following Hurricane Katrina's arrival marked a tragic NADIR for millions of people living in Louisiana, Mississippi, and many Gulf Coast communities. The Gulf Oil Spill marked yet another tragic NADIR for the region as hundreds of millions of gallons of oil DESPOILED (ravaged) once PRISTINE (Word 383) beaches and wetlands.

Testing Your Vocabulary

Each SAT contains 19 sentence completion questions that are primarily a test of your vocabulary. Each sentence completion will always have a key word or phrase that will lead you to the correct answer. Use the vocabulary from Chapters 1-4 to circle the answer to each of the following 10 sentence completion questions. You'll find answers and explanations on pages 111 to 112.

1. The head coach responded to the breach of team rules by instituting unusually strict rules that players felt were too _____.

    (A) cryptic
    (B) diminutive
    (C) draconian
    (D) jocular
    (E) nebulous

2. Outraged editors charged the vice-principal with _____ their work by deleting key parts of a controversial article on teenage drinking.

    (A) coveting
    (B) lauding
    (C) bowdlerizing
    (D) ostracizing
    (E) gerrymandering

3. As a result of the disastrous hurricane, Lindsey was left both _____ and _____: she lost all of her possessions, and she faced a seemingly hopeless series of problems.

    (A) affluent .. exuberant
    (B) maudlin .. contemplative
    (C) nostalgic .. laconic
    (D) galvanized .. energized
    (E) impecunious .. desperate

4. Morgan was _____ person, naturally inclined to be tearful and excessively sentimental.

    (A) a quixotic
    (B) a recalcitrant
    (C) an amicable
    (D) a deft
    (E) a maudlin

5. Ryan missed the essay's main theme, focusing instead on trivial details that could only be described as _____.

    (A) picayune
    (B) intemperate
    (C) implausible
    (D) anachronistic
    (E) prodigious

6. Some people alternate between contrasting temperaments; either they are _____ or they are _____.

    (A) nefarious .. wicked
    (B) morose .. despondent
    (C) affable .. genial
    (D) quixotic .. pragmatic
    (E) jovial .. jocular

7. Sydney is best described as a _____: she is an independent person who recognizes that the majority is sometimes wrong.

    (A) martinet
    (B) maverick
    (C) stoic
    (D) charlatan
    (E) ascetic

8. There was _____ when the Jonas Brothers' concert began: fans screamed so loudly that few in the arena could hear the lyrics of their songs.

    (A) serendipity
    (B) sophistry
    (C) pandemonium
    (D) ambivalence
    (E) anguish

9. The new highway proved to be _____: it suffered from expensive cost over-runs and failed to relieve traffic congestion.

    (A) an impasse
    (B) a boon
    (C) a dirge
    (D) a conjecture
    (E) a debacle

10. Charlie looked back on his family's vacation at the lake as _____ time filled with carefree days and untroubled tranquility.

    (A) a halcyon
    (B) an anguished
    (C) a divisive
    (D) an intemperate
    (E) an ambiguous

Answers and Explanations

1. **C**

   The question asks you to find a word that describes the "strict rules" instituted by the head coach. The correct answer is DRACONIAN (Word 131).

2. **C**

   The question asks you to find a word that means "deleting key parts." The correct answer is BOWDLERIZING (Word 147).

3. **E**

   The question asks you to find a first word that describes Lindsey's condition after losing "all of her possessions" and a second word that is consistent with the key word "hopeless." The correct answer is IMPECUNIOUS (Word 138) and DESPERATE.

4. **E**

   The question asks you to find a word that means to be "naturally inclined to be tearful and excessively sentimental." The correct answer is MAUDLIN (Word 142).

5. **A**

   The question asks you to find a word that means "focusing on trivial details." The correct answer is PICAYUNE (Word 149).

6. D

The question asks you to find a pair of antonyms describing "contrasting temperaments." Choices A, B, C and E are all pairs of synonyms. Only choice D provides a pair of antonyms. The correct answer is therefore QUIXOTIC (WORD 143) and PRAGMATIC (Word 12).

7. B

The question asks you to find a word describing "an independent person" who doesn't always follow the majority. The correct answer is MAVERICK (Word 151).

8. C

The question asks you to find a word describing a concert in which fans "screamed so loudly that few could hear the lyrics." The correct answer is PANDEMONIUM (Word 144).

9. E

The question asks you to find a word describing a highway extension that was expensive, inadequate, and noisy. In short, the highway extension was a complete failure. The correct answer is therefore DEBACLE (Word 146).

10. A

The question asks you to find a word that is consistent with "carefree days and untroubled tranquility." The correct answer is HALCYON (Word 134).

Chapter 5

THE MIGHTY PREFIX WORDS: 156–200

A prefix is a word part placed before a root in order to direct or change the root's meaning. Prefixes are short but mighty. A knowledge of prefixes can help you unlock the meaning of difficult SAT words. Many vocabulary books contain long lists of Latin and Greek prefixes. Many like *anti* (against), *sub* (under), and *multi* (many) are well-known and obvious. Still others like *peri* (around) generate few if any words tested on the SAT. This chapter will focus upon five sets of the most widely-used prefixes on the SAT. Learning them is thus of paramount, or vital, importance. We will also study words ending with the suffix OUS. It is by far the most important and useful suffix on the SAT.

A. E AND EX: THE MIGHTY PREFIXES E AND EX TELL YOU THAT THINGS ARE GOING OUT

The prefixes E and EX are UBIQUITOUS (everywhere). You are familiar with them in everyday words such as exit, extinguish, and erase. The prefixes E and EX always mean OUT. Here are seven frequently used SAT words that begin with the prefixes E and EX.

156. EXPUNGE, EXCISE, EXPURGATE:
All three mean to take OUT; delete; remove

In the movie *300*, Xerxes threatened to EXPUNGE all memory of Sparta and Leonidas: "Every piece of Greek parchment shall be burned, every Greek historian and every Greek scribe shall have his eyes put out and his thumbs cut off. Ultimately the very name of Sparta or Leonidas will be punishable by death. The world will never know you existed."

Xerxes failed to carry out his threat to EXCISE the names of Sparta and King Leonidas from the historic record. However, a powerful Egyptian Pharaoh, Thutmose III, did succeed in EXPURGATING his mother, Hatshepsut's, name from Egyptian monuments. A female pharaoh, Hatshepsut reigned for nearly twenty years in the 15th century BCE. Possibly motivated by jealousy, Thutmose ruthlessly defaced his mother's monuments and EXPURGATED her name from historic records. All memory of Hatshepsut was lost until 19th century Egyptologists rediscovered her monuments and restored her place in history.

157. ECCENTRIC:
Literally OUT of the center; departing from a recognized, conventional, or established norm; an odd, UNCONVENTIONAL (Word 7) person

Do you remember Doctor Emmett L. Brown in the *Back to the Future* movies? Doc Brown was the inventor of the DeLorean time machine. Most of the people in Hill Valley regarded him as a strange and ECCENTRIC "mad scientist." Doc Brown did indeed have a number of ECCENTRICITIES. He often enunciated his words with wide-eyed facial expressions and broad gestures. Doc always tried to use a big word rather than a small one. For example, he referred to a dance as a "rhythmic, ceremonial ritual."

158. EXTRICATE:
To get OUT of a difficult situation or entanglement

Have you ever had to EXTRICATE yourself from an embarrassing situation? If so, you are not alone. In the movie *School of Rock*, Dewey Finn had to EXTRICATE himself from the embarrassing situation he created by impersonating his friend and claiming to be a certified elementary substitute teacher.

EXTRICATING yourself from a lie is embarrassing. However, being EXTRICATED from an automobile crash can be a matter of life or death. Fortunately, emergency workers have a number of tools specially designed to help EXTRICATE injured people from car wrecks and small spaces. These cutters, spreaders, and rams are collectively called "Jaws of Life."

159. EXEMPLARY:
Standing OUT from the norm; outstanding; worthy of imitation

Have you ever been praised for writing an EXEMPLARY report, giving an EXEMPLARY answer or designing an EXEMPLARY project? If so, you should be proud of yourself. EXEMPLARY means to be outstanding and thus worthy of imitation. Recording artists and actors are recognized for their EXEMPLARY performances by receiving a VMA Moonman, a Grammy, or an Oscar. Scientists and writers are honored for their EXEMPLARY work by receiving a Nobel Prize.

160. ENUMERATE:
To count OUT; to list; to tick off the reasons for

What do Thomas Jefferson, the author of the Declaration of Independence, and Kat, the fictional character in *10 Things I Hate About You*, have in common? Both felt compelled to ENUMERATE the reasons for an action. In the Declaration of Independence, Jefferson ENUMERATED reasons why the colonies declared their independence from Great Britain. In a poem she read to her literature class, Kat ENUMERATED ten reasons why she claimed to "hate" Patrick.

161. ELUSIVE:
OUT of reach and therefore difficult to catch, define, or describe

Gossip Girl is an OMNISCIENT (all-knowing) yet ELUSIVE blogger who narrates the lives of a group of wealthy Upper East Side teenagers. Each episode begins with Gossip Girl's whispered voice asking, "And who am I?" But the ELUSIVE Gossip Girl refuses to reveal her identify, insisting, "That's something I'll never tell." Although Chuck, Serena, and Blair have repeatedly attempted to discover Gossip Girl's identity, their efforts have been FUTILE (Word 46). Gossip Girl remains an ELUSIVE and unseen presence in their lives.

162. EXORBITANT:
Literally OUT of orbit and therefore unreasonably expensive

The new Dallas Cowboys Stadium is proof that not only are things bigger in Texas, they are also more EXORBITANT! The new stadium features 300 luxury suites costing between $100,000 and $500,000 a year with a 20-year lease. Although this may seem GRANDIOSE (pretentious) to average fans, the suites provide "the ultimate football experience" by featuring limestone floors, private restrooms, and a special parking lot. The reserved parking is a COVETED (Word 32) feature. Parking is limited at Cowboys Stadium. As a result, regular football fans will pay $75 for parking, a price many are calling EXORBITANT.

B. RE: THE MIGHTY PREFIX RE TELLS YOU THAT THINGS ARE COMING BACK AGAIN AND AGAIN

The prefix RE means BACK or AGAIN. You are familiar with it in everyday words such as REPEAT, REWIND, and REVERSE. Here are ten SAT words that begin with the prefix RE:

163. REPUDIATE, RECANT, RENOUNCE:
All three mean to take BACK; to reject; DISAVOW

"Martin, do you or do you not REPUDIATE these books and the falsehoods they contain?" The place was the Diet of Worms. The time was April 1521. The question posed by the papal legate Johann Eck required an answer. For Martin Luther, the moment of truth had finally arrived. How would Luther respond?

Luther refused to REPUDIATE his words, defiantly declaring, "I cannot, I will not RECANT these words. For to do so is to go against conscience. Here I stand!" Luther's courageous refusal to RENOUNCE his beliefs helped spark the Protestant Reformation.

164. REDUNDANT:
Needlessly repetitive; saying things AGAIN and AGAIN

What do Justin Bieber and SAT teachers have in common? Both are REDUNDANT when they emphasize a key point. In his hit song *Baby*, JB REDUNDANTLY repeats the word "baby" an amazing 57 times. No wonder the song sticks in your mind! SAT teachers are also purposefully REDUNDANT when they IMPLORE (urge) their students to study the vocabulary words in *Direct Hits*. Here's why: a level 1 and 2 vocabulary will only enable you to achieve a critical reading score of about 450. You will need a level 3 vocabulary to achieve a score of about 580. And finally, you will need a level 4 and 5 vocabulary to score 600 and up. So now you know why SAT teachers are so REDUNDANT. Study your *Direct Hits* vocabulary.

Tip for a Direct Hit

Don't be alarmed if you see the word REDUNDANCY on your SAT. It usually refers to the duplication or repetition of equipment needed to provide a backup in case the primary systems fail. For example, scuba equipment includes a REDUNDANT regulator in case there is a problem with the main air regulator. This REDUNDANCY is an important safety precaution.

165. RELINQUISH:

To give something BACK; to surrender or give BACK a possession, right, or privilege

In the movie *Enchanted*, Queen Narissa's foremost goal is to keep her crown. However, if the marriage between Prince Edward and Giselle takes place, Giselle will become Andalasia's new queen, forcing Narissa to RELINQUISH her crown. The villainous Narissa will do anything to prevent the marriage so that she will not have to RELINQUISH her power.

166. RESILIENT:

To leap BACK; to come BACK from ADVERSITY or misfortune

Amy's long wait for her SAT scores finally ended. She nervously accessed her College Board account, and then as the numbers appeared on her computer screen, her heart sank. Amy's scores were not as good as she had hoped. What would Amy do? Would she make excuses and give up? Or would she be

RESILIENT and bounce back from a temporary setback? Amy chose to study even harder. Her RESILIENCE worked. Amy's SAT scores shot up, and she received a scholarship to her top college choice.

Amy's story can be your story. The SAT is a challenging test. Don't be discouraged if your first results are not what you hoped for. Stay focused, study hard, and be RESILIENT!

167. REAFFIRM:
To assert AGAIN; to confirm; state positively

Given at the height of the Cold War, John F. Kennedy's Inaugural Address REAFFIRMED his commitment to freedom when he pledged that America would "pay any price, bear any burden, meet any hardship, support any friend, oppose any foe to assure the survival and success of liberty." Given at the height of the Civil Rights Movement, Dr. King's "I Have A Dream" speech REAFFIRMED his faith in the American dream when he proclaimed, "I have a dream that my four little children will one day live in a nation where they will be judged not by the color of their skin but by the content of their character."

168. RETICENT:
To hold BACK one's thoughts, feelings and personal affairs; restrained or reserved

Have you seen the opening scene in *High School Musical*? While minding their own business at a New Year's Eve party, Troy and Gabriella are randomly chosen to participate in a karaoke contest. Both are RETICENT about participating. But fate has other plans for them. As they soon discover, this is the "start of something new!"

169. REBUFF:
To repel or drive BACK; to bluntly reject

In the movie *Superman Returns*, Lois Lane REBUFFED Superman when she wrote an article entitled, "Why the World Doesn't Need Superman." In the movie *Clueless*, Cher claimed that Mr. Hall "brutally REBUFFED" her plea to raise her debate grade. And Amy Winehouse has remained RECALCITRANT (Word 15) as she repeatedly REBUFFS pleas from her family and friends to seek help for her smoking and drug problems.

170. RENOVATE:
To make new AGAIN; restore by repairing and remodeling

Nov is a Latin root meaning "new." RENOVATE thus means to make new again. Hurricane Katrina caused extensive damage in New Orleans and Biloxi, Mississippi. Business and community leaders in both cities have vowed to undertake extensive RENOVAT-ION projects that will restore damaged neighborhoods and revive tourism. For example, in 2007, actor Brad Pitt commissioned 13 architecture firms to submit designs for homes to help RENOVATE New Orleans' IMPOVERISHED (Word 231) Lower Ninth Ward. The project, called *Make It Right*, calls for building 150 affordable, environmentally-sound homes by 2010.

171. REJUVENATE:

To make young AGAIN; to restore youthful vigor and appearance

REJUVENATE is an enticing word. Everyone wants to look and feel young. Health spas promise to REJUVENATE exhausted muscles, shampoos promise to REJUVENATE tired hair, and herbal medicines promise to REJUVENATE worn-out immune systems.

 Tip for a Direct Hit

The word REJUVENATE is easy to remember. It is formed by combining the prefix *re* meaning again and the Latin root *juvenis* meaning young. So REJUVENATE literally means to be young again.

172. RESURGENT:

To rise AGAIN; to sweep or surge BACK

Apple Computer was founded by Steve Jobs on April 1, 1976. After great initial success, the company suffered crippling financial losses. As a result, the company's Board of Directors ousted Jobs in 1985. But both Jobs and Apple proved to be RESILIENT (Word 166). Jobs returned to Apple in 1997. Under his leadership, the RESURGENT company introduced a series of INNOVATIVE (Word 126) products that included the iPod, iPhone, and the iPad. The company's Macintosh computer also experienced a RESURGENCE in popularity when Jobs made the decision to equip it with powerful x86 processors made by Intel.

C. DE: THE MIGHTY PREFIX DE TELLS YOU THAT THINGS ARE HEADED DOWN, DOWN, DOWN

The prefix DE means DOWN. You are familiar with DE in such everyday words as DEMOLISH, DE-CLINE, and DEPRESS. Here are eight SAT words that begin with the prefix DE:

173. DELETERIOUS:
Going DOWN in the sense of having a harmful effect; injurious

What do you think is the fastest growing cause of disease and death in America? The surprising and tragic answer is obesity. As a result of being SEDENT-ARY (lacking physical activity) and practicing unhealthy eating habits, an UNPRECEDENTED (Word 259) number of Americans are carrying excess body weight. This excess weight can have a number of DELETERIOUS effects, including increases in heart disease, asthma, and diabetes.

174. DECRY:
To put DOWN in the sense of openly condemning; to express strong disapproval

During the 1920s, American novelists such as Sinclair Lewis DECRIED the era's rampant materialism and conformity. Three decades later, Jack Kerouac and other Beat Generation writers also DECRIED sterile middle-class conformity while celebrating spontaneous individualism and creativity.

175. DESPONDENT:
Feeling DOWNCAST; very dejected; FORLORN

What do Danielle (*Ever After*) and Giselle (*Enchanted*) have in common? Although both Danielle and Giselle ultimately found true love, both also experienced the pain of being DESPONDENT. After being abruptly rejected by Prince Henry, Danielle fled to her home and sat crying on the front step. She was truly DESPONDENT – sad, lonely, and deserted by her true love. Giselle also experienced what it is like to be DESPONDENT when a New York City beggar stole her tiara and left her crying alone in the pouring rain.

176. DENOUNCE:
To put DOWN in the sense of a making a
formal accusation; to speak against

The pages of history contain a number of inspiring examples of brave individuals who DENOUNCED corruption, tyranny and moral abuses. For example, Voltaire DENOUNCED the Old Regime, William Lloyd Garrison DENOUNCED slavery, Rachel Carson DENOUNCED the use of chemical pesticides, and Nelson Mandela DENOUNCED apartheid.

177. DEMISE:
To go all the way DOWN in the sense of ending
by death; the cessation of existence or activity

What do the dinosaurs and the Whig Party have in common? Both met with a sudden and unexpected DEMISE. Paleontologists now believe that a giant asteroid struck the Earth about 65 million years ago, causing the DEMISE of the dinosaurs and many other plants and animals. Historians point out that the Kansas-Nebraska Act of 1854 brought about the final

DEMISE of the Whig Party while at the same time sparking the rise of the Republican Party. Note that the word DEMISE is formed by combining the prefix *de* meaning down with the Latin root *misi* meaning "to send." So DEMISE literally means "to send down."

178. DEBUNK:
To put DOWN by exposing false and exaggerated claims

Kanye West is a successful recording artist whose career was TARNISHED (diminished) when he took the microphone away from Taylor Swift at the 2009 MTV Video Music Awards and proclaimed that Beyoncé's video *Single Ladies* was "one of the best videos of all time." Fortunately, Grand Master Larry (aka your author) totally DEBUNKED Kanye's TACTLESS (inconsiderate) behavior in his "hit" single GML rapped :

> *Kanye, you COVET attention and fame,*
> *But you are ruining your name.*
> *You're often TACTLESS, and rude,*
> *Interrupting Taylor was crude.*
> *You're easy to DEBUNK,*
> *Cause your attitude is junk!*

179. DERIDE:
To put DOWN with contemptuous jeering; to ridicule or laugh at

In the movie *Happy Gilmore*, Shooter McGavin DERIDED Happy as an incompetent NOVICE (Word 119) who did not know how to putt. DERISION is not limited to the movies. New artistic styles have often been DERIDED by both the public and critics. For example, Edouard Manet's painting *Luncheon on the*

THE MIGHTY PREFIX WORDS: 156 – 200

Grass provoked a storm of scorn and DERISION. Hostile critics DERIDED Manet calling him an "apostle of the ugly and repulsive."

180. DEVOID:
To go DOWN in the sense of being empty; completely lacking in substance or quality; BEREFT

What was the worst movie you have ever seen? Why did you select this movie? You probably chose the movie because it was DEVOID of humor, plot, and acting. Here is a list of movies that were panned by critics for being DEVOID of all redeeming value: *Battlefield Earth, Gigli, Godzilla, From Justin to Kelly, Glitter*, and *Speed Racer*.

D. IM, IN AND IR: THESE MIGHTY LATIN PREFIXES ALL TELL YOU NO OR NOT

The prefixes IM, IN, and IR all mean NO or NOT. You are familiar with these prefixes in everyday words such as IMMATURE, INCOMPETENT and IRREPLACABLE. Here are six SAT words that begin with the prefixes IM, IN, or IR:

181. IMPECCABLE:
Having NO flaws; perfect

Look closely at the word IMPECCABLE. The prefix IM means no and the Latin verb *peccare* means "to sin." So the word IMPECCABLE literally means to have no sin and thus to be flawless or perfect.

Do you open doors for your girlfriend and say "yes, sir" and "yes, ma-am" when speaking to adults? If so, you are demonstrating IMPECCABLE manners. Do

Page 126   Chapter 5

you complete your homework assignments in advance and study for all your tests? If so, you are demonstrating IMPECCABLE judgment. Whether manners or judgment, IMPECCABLE always means flawless.

182. IMPLACABLE:
NOT capable of being placated or appeased

In his quest to fight for "truth, justice, and the American way," Superman must defeat Lex Luther and other IMPLACABLE foes. Superman is not alone in his struggle against IMPLACABLE villains. Spider-Man must defeat the Green Goblin, and Batman's most IMPLACABLE enemy is the Joker.

Like superheroes, modern nations can also have IMPLACABLE enemies. For example, the United States and al Qaeda are IMPLACABLE enemies locked in a deadly struggle that cannot be avoided.

183. INEXORABLE:
NOT capable of being stopped; relentless; inevitable

Although it was a luxury liner, the Titanic did not have the advanced warning systems that modern ships have today. The Titanic did have six lookout guards who stood in the crow's nest and kept a VIGILANT (watchful, alert) lookout for passing icebergs that could endanger the ship. At 11:40 PM, Frederick Fleet suddenly spotted an iceberg directly in the ship's path. Fleet urgently informed the bridge, and frantic officers ordered emergency maneuvers. But the ship was traveling too fast. It was on an INEXORABLE course to hit the iceberg. The Titanic sank two hours and forty minutes after Fleet's fateful warning.

184. INCOHERENT:

NOT coherent and therefore lacking organization; lacking logical or meaningful connections

Do you remember Cher's INCOHERENT speech at the beginning of "Clueless"? Here it is in all of its IN-COHERENT glory:

> *Mr Hall*: Should all oppressed people be allowed refuge in America? Cher, two minutes.
>
> *Cher*:   So okay, like right now for example the Haitians need to come to America. But some people are all what about the strain on our resources. It's like when I had a garden party for my father's birthday, right? I said RSVP because it was a sit-down dinner. But people came that like did not RSVP. So I was like totally upset. I had to dash to the kitchen, rearrange the food, and squish in some extra place settings. But by the end of the day, it was the more the merrier. And so, if the government could just get to the kitchen and re-arrange some things, we can certainly party with the Haitians. And in con-clusion, may I remind you that it does not say RSVP on the Statue of Liberty.

185. INSURMOUNTABLE:

NOT capable of being surmounted or overcome

Beginning in the 1850s, far-seeing American leaders dreamed of building a transcontinental railroad that would bind the nation together. But SKEPTICS (Word

102) argued that while the railroad was a worthy goal, it would face a series of INSURMOUNTABLE obstacles that included hostile Plains Indians and the towering, snow-clogged Sierra Nevada mountains. Crews, which at times included over 15,000 workers, repelled the Indians and blasted tunnels through the mountains. The once INSURMOUNTABLE task was completed when Leland Stanford used a silver sledge-hammer to drive in the golden spike on May 10, 1869.

186. IRREVERENT:

Lacking proper respect or seriousness; disrespectful

The writers of the Simpsons and Comedy Central PUNDIT (Word 117) Stephen Colbert are well-known for their IRREVERENT jokes and witticisms. In the Simpsons movie, a message on one of Springfield's church marquees reads, "Thou shalt turn off thy cell phone." In his IRREVERENT book *I Am America (And So Can You!)*, Colbert provides a sample of a college essay featuring the overuse of a thesaurus ("the APEX (Word 154), pinnacle, acme, vertex, and ZENITH (Word 154) of my life's experiences") and the false claim that his great-great-uncle's name is on a building at Dartmouth.

E.   CIRCU: THIS MIGHTY PREFIX TELLS YOU THAT WHAT GOES AROUND COMES AROUND

The prefix CIRCU means AROUND. You are familiar with it in everyday words such as CIRCUMFER-ENCE, CIRCUIT, and CIRCULATION. Here are four SAT words that begin with the prefix CIRCU:

187. CIRCUMSPECT:

To look carefully around and therefore to be cautious and careful; PRUDENT

Would you describe yourself as someone who likes to be the first to buy a new electronic device and be the first to wear a new fashion to school? Or do you prefer to take a wait-and-see approach to new inventions and styles? If you prefer to wait and see, you are being CIRCUMSPECT. A CIRCUMSPECT person prefers to be cautious and look before he or she leaps.

188. CIRCUITOUS:

CIRCULAR and therefore indirect in language, behavior or action

In the movie *National Treasure: Book of Secrets*, Benjamin Franklin Gates' great-great grandfather is suddenly implicated as a key conspirator in Abraham Lincoln's death. Determined to prove his ancestor's innocence, Ben follows a chain of clues that takes him on a CIRCUITOUS chase that begins in Paris and then takes him to Buckingham Palace in London, the White House, a secret tunnel under Mount Vernon, the Library of Congress, and finally Mount Rushmore. This CIRCUITOUS journey leads Ben and his crew to uncover a number of startling revelations and secrets.

189. CIRCUMVENT:

To circle AROUND and therefore bypass; to avoid by artful maneuvering

During the 1920s, Al Capone and other gangsters built profitable illegal businesses by CIRCUMVENTING prohibition laws. Today, illegal businesses continue to CIRCUMVENT our laws. For example, drug lords annually smuggle over 100 tons of cocaine and other illegal drugs into the United States.

It is also possible for a nation to CIRCUMVENT international law. Iran signed the Nuclear Non-Proliferation Treaty in 1970. Nonetheless, many believe that the Iranian government is now CIRCUM-VENTING its international agreements by secretly developing a program to build nuclear weapons.

190. CIRCUMSCRIBE:
To draw a line AROUND and therefore to narrowly limit or restrict actions

What do Juliet (*Romeo and Juliet*), Janie Crawford (*Their Eyes Were Watching God*), and Viola Hastings (*She's The Man*) have in common? Although they lived in very different times and places, all faced restrictions that CIRCUMSCRIBED their freedom. Juliet wanted to live with Romeo but couldn't because her family CIRCUMSCRIBED her freedom by insisting she marry Count Paris. Janie wanted to socialize with a variety of people but couldn't because her husband CIRCUMSCRIBED her freedom by refusing to let her participate in the rich social life that occurred on the front porch of their general store. And Viola wanted to try out for the boys soccer team but couldn't because the coach CIRCUMSCRIBED her freedom by contending that girls aren't good enough to play with boys.

F. OUS: THIS ALL-IMPORTANT SUFFIX MEANS FILLED WITH

The suffix OUS means filled with. You are familiar with it in everyday words such as JOYOUS,

COURAGEOUS, and POISONOUS. Here are ten SAT words that end with the suffix OUS:

191. MAGNANIMOUS:
Filled with generosity and forgiveness; forgoing resentment and revenge

On first glance, MAGNANIMOUS looks like a "big" and difficult SAT word. But looks can be deceiving. Let's use our knowledge of prefixes, roots, and the suffix OUS to divide and conquer MAGNANIMOUS!

The prefix *magna* is easy to recognize. It means "big" as in the word magnify. The root *anim* comes from the Latin *animex* meaning breath or soul. An animal is thus a living, breathing thing, and an inanimate object lacks a spirit. And finally, the suffix *OUS* means "is filled with." So MAGNANIMOUS literally means filled with a great spirit and therefore generous and forgiving. For example, following Lee's surrender at Appomattox, Grant MAGNANIMOUSLY allowed the Confederate officers to keep their side arms and permitted soldiers to keep personal horses and mules. The Union troops then MAGNANIMOUSLY saluted as their defeated foes paraded past them.

192. ERRONEOUS:
Filled with errors; wrong

Lil Wayne's PENCHANT (Word 62) for tattoos is well known. Fascinated fans have deciphered the meaning of most of Wheezy's MYRIAD (Word 323) tats. However, the three teardrops on his face remain a source of controversy. Many believe that they represent people Lil Wayne has killed. This belief is ERRONEOUS and totally UNCORROBORATED (unsupported). In his song "Hustler Musik," Wheezy clearly states that he has never killed anyone. The three tear-drops actually represent family members who have been killed.

193. MOMENTOUS:
Filled with importance; very significant

In 1960, lunch counters throughout the South remained segregated. While moderates urged patience, Joe McNeil and three other black college students disagreed. Calling segregation "evil pure and simple," the four students sat down at a Woolworth's lunch counter in Greensboro, NC, and ordered coffee and apple pie. Although the waitress refused to serve them, the students remained STEADFAST (fixed, unswerving) in their determination to desegregate the dining area. Now known as the Greensboro Four, the students ultimately prevailed. The sit-in movement begun by the Greensboro Four had MOMENTOUS consequences. Just four years later, the Civil Rights Act of 1964 MANDATED (ordered) desegregation in all public places.

194. MELLIFLUOUS:
Smooth and sweet; flowing like honey

Let's divide and conquer the seemingly difficult SAT word, MELLIFLUOUS. The Latin roots *mel* meaning "honey" and *fluus* meaning "to flow" are the key to understanding MELLIFLUOUS. MELLIFLUOUS is literally filled with flowing honey. It almost always is used to describe singers who have a sweet-sounding voice. For example, Smokey Robinson, Marvin Gaye, Otis Redding, and Usher are all renowned for their smooth, MELLIFLUOUS voices.

195. OMINOUS:
Filled with menace; threatening

An omen is a sign indicating that something good or bad will happen. The word OMINOUS is filled with bad omens that PORTEND (foretell) the imminent arrival of something that will be both menacing and threatening. For example, scientists warn that melting glaciers, rising sea levels, and rising temperatures are all OMINOUS signs that global warming is getting worse at an alarming rate.

196. ACRIMONIOUS:
Filled with bitterness; sharpness in words; RANCOROUS

What do the words ACID and ACRIMONIOUS have in common? Both are derived from the Latin adjective *acer* meaning "sharp" or "bitter." Acid is sharp or bitter to taste, while ACRIMONIOUS refers to sharp and bitter words.

Celebrity divorces often degenerate into ACRI-MONIOUS contests over money and child custody. While the couples do not throw acid at each other, they often don't hesitate to hurl ACRIMONIOUS accusations at their spouses. For example, Denise Richards alleged that Charlie Sheen was "unfaithful and abusive" while Britney called Kevin Federline "the biggest mistake I've ever made." Needless to say, celebrity magazines are only too happy to CHRON-ICLE (record) all the ACRIMONIOUS allegations made by the stars and their lawyers.

Tip for a Direct Hit

The words ACERBIC, ACUTE, and EXACERBATE also contain the Latin adjective *acer*. ACERBIC refers to the sharp wit often displayed by acid-tongued critics. ACUTE refers to a sharp feeling or sense as an ACUTE sense of smell. EXACERBATE (Word 251) means to make a problem sharper and thus worse.

197. COPIOUS:
Filled with abundance; plentiful

What do the Greek god Zeus, the Thanksgiving horn of plenty, the SAT word COPIOUS, and Fall Out Boy's Pete Wentz have in common? According to Greek mythology, the cornucopia refers to the horn of a goat that nursed Zeus. The horn had supernatural powers and soon became a symbol of fertility and plenty. In America, the cornucopia has come to be associated with the Thanksgiving harvest. The SAT word COPIOUS is derived from the Latin word *copia* meaning plenty, so COPIOUS means filled with plenty and abundant. What does all this have to do with Pete Wentz? Like many rock stars, Pete Wentz wears COPIOUS amounts of eyeliner, known as guyliner!

198. ABSTEMIOUS:
Filled with moderation; temperate in eating and drinking

Abs is a Latin prefix meaning "away or off." For example, absent students are away from school. The

Latin word *temetum* means an intoxicating drink. So if you are ABSTEMIOUS, you are filled with a desire to stay away from strong drinks. Today, an ABSTEMIOUS person is also moderate in eating.

199. MALODOROUS:
Filled with an unpleasant odor; foul smelling

What do stink bugs and skunks have in common? Both can emit a MALODOROUS smell. If disturbed, stink bugs emit a liquid whose MALODOROUS smell is due to cyanide compounds. Skunks are notorious for their MALODOROUS scent glands that emit a highly offensive smell that is usually described as a combination of the odors of rotten eggs, garlic, and burnt rubber. The skunk's MALODOROUS smell is a defensive weapon that repels predators and can be detected up to a mile away.

200. TEDIOUS:
Filled with boredom; very tiresome; dull and fatiguing

What do studying long lists of SAT vocabulary words and taking SAT practice tests have in common? Most students find these tasks very TEDIOUS. *Direct Hits* is designed to make studying vocabulary much less TEDIOUS. In fact, we hope that you have found Volume 1 to be an interesting learning experience that has achieved our goal of helping you become more articulate. As an articulate person, you will be able to speak more eloquently, write more convincingly, and, of course, score more successfully on your SAT!

Testing Your Vocabulary

Each SAT contains 19 sentence completion questions that are primarily a test of your vocabulary. Each sentence completion will always have a key word or phrase that will lead you to the correct answer. Use the vocabulary from Chapters 1-5 to circle the answer to each of the following 11 sentence completion questions. You'll find answers and explanations on pages 141 to 143.

1. Unfortunately, the zoo's new pandas were _____: they remained very shy and were reluctant to acknowledge visitors.

    (A) extroverted
    (B) reticent
    (C) incoherent
    (D) irreverent
    (E) itinerant

2. The Mayan's sudden and irrevocable _____ is a long-standing historic _____: over the years, scholars have suggested a number of possible causes, including excessive warfare and devastating natural disasters, to explain the disappearance of Mayan civilization.

    (A) demise .. mystery
    (B) longevity .. enigma
    (C) rebirth .. riddle
    (D) collapse .. myth
    (E) resurgence .. conjecture

3. Scientists warn that the _____ consequences of global warming will not be limited to the deterioration of penguin and polar bear habitats; humans can also expect devastating hurricanes and _____ floods.

    (A) fortuitous .. damaging
    (B) fleeting .. prodigious
    (C) painstaking .. beneficial
    (D) incontrovertible .. innocuous
    (E) deleterious .. destructive

4. Muckrakers like Upton Sinclair and Ida Tarbell _____ the corrupt business practices of early 20th century robber barons, _____ their unbridled greed and indifferent attitude toward the public good.

    (A) disapproved .. lauding
    (B) extolled .. disparaging
    (C) reaffirmed .. deriding
    (D) celebrated .. censuring
    (E) decried .. denouncing

5. Cautious, conventional, and always careful to follow procedures, Matthew is the very model of a _____ government bureaucrat.

    (A) audacious
    (B) resilient
    (C) circumspect
    (D) sardonic
    (E) maudlin

6. Claire was both envied and renowned for her faultless manners, refined taste, and _____ sense of decorum.

    (A) vulgar
    (B) incoherent
    (C) impeccable
    (D) obsolete
    (E) irreverent

7. Far from draining their energy, the challenge posed by the Tournament of Champions seems to have _____ the coach and his previously-indifferent team.

    (A) rejuvenated
    (B) polarized
    (C) circumscribed
    (D) depleted
    (E) bored

8. What is the most inspiring about Professor DeMarco's portrayal of Venetian life is the _____ of the human spirit, the force that has sustained the island-city through adversity and always remains undaunted.

    (A) divisiveness
    (B) resilience
    (C) superficiality
    (D) reticence
    (E) callousness

9. The debate between the candidates was animated but _____, since the speakers needlessly repeated campaign slogans and innocuous promises.

    (A) eccentric
    (B) sarcastic
    (C) unconventional
    (D) serene
    (E) redundant

10. Jessica's report was criticized for being both _____ and _____: it was poorly organized and overly vague.

    (A) meticulous .. ambiguous
    (B) circuitous .. adroit
    (C) incoherent .. nebulous
    (D) glib .. poignant
    (E) inexorable .. dismissive

11. Gustave Courbet's bitter and spiteful denunciations of his critics earned him a reputation for being _____.

    (A) magnanimous
    (B) abstemious
    (C) meticulous
    (D) acrimonious
    (E) erroneous

Answers and Explanations

1. B

The question asks you to find a word that best describes "shy" pandas that are "reluctant to acknowledge visitors." The correct answer is RETICENT (Word 168).

2. A

The question asks you to find a pair of words that are consistent with the Mayan's "disappearance" and the fact that scholars still cannot explain why they vanished. The correct answer is DEMISE (Word 177) and MYSTERY.

3. E

The question asks you to find a pair of negative words that are consistent with the key words "deterioration" and "devastating." The correct answer is DELETERIOUS (Word 173) and DESTRUCTIVE. Note that DESTRUCTIVE is consistent with "devastating" and that the consequences of global warming are DELETERIOUS for both animals and humans.

4. E

The question asks you to find a pair of words describing how muckrakers would respond to robber barons who are described as "corrupt," greedy, and "indifferent to the public good." Choices A, B, C, and D all include both positive and negative words. Since the sentence calls for a logically consistent pair of negative words, the correct answer is DECRIED (WORD 174) and DENOUNCING (Word 176).

5. **C**

The question asks you to find a word that describes a bureaucrat who is "cautious, conventional, and always careful to follow procedures." The correct answer is CIRCUMSPECT (Word 187).

6. **C**

The question asks you to find a word that is consistent with having "faultless manner" and "refined taste." The correct answer is IMPECCABLE (Word 181).

7. **A**

The question asks you to find a word that describes the impact the Tournament of Champions had upon a "coach and his previously indifferent team." It is important to note that the competition did not "drain their energy." The correct answer is REJUVENATE (Word 171) since it contrasts with both the phrases "draining their energy" and "previously indifferent."

8. **B**

The question asks you to find a word that best describes the spirit of the Venetians. You are told that this spirit or force sustained the Venetians through "adversity and always remains un-daunted." The correct answer is RESILIENCE (Word 166).

9. **E**

The question asks you to find a word that means "needlessly repeated." The correct answer is REDUNDANT (Word 164).

10. **C**

The question asks you to find a first word that means "poorly organized" and a second word that means "overly vague." The correct answer is INCOHERENT (Word 184) and NEBULOUS (Word 59).

11. **D**

The question asks you to find a negative word that best characterizes how Courbet's "bitter and spiteful denunciations" affected his reputation. The correct answer is ACRIMONIOUS (Word 196).

Fast Review

Quick Definitions

Volume 1 contains 200 words each of which is illustrated with vivid pop culture and historic examples. The Fast Review is designed to provide you with an easy and efficient way to review each of these words. I recommend that you put a check beside each word that you know. That way you can quickly identify the words you are having trouble remembering. Focus on each hard to remember word by going over its definition, reviewing its examples, and by trying to come up with your own memory tip. For example, Word 50, FORTITUDE begins with the word FORT. Now visualize a military fort. Is your fort manned by troops and protected by cannons? Good! Since FORT means strong, FORTITUDE also includes the idea of strength. FORTITUDE refers to the strength of mind that enables a person to encounter danger or adversity with courage.

Good luck with your review. Remember, don't expect to learn all of these words at once. Frequent repetition is the best way to learn and remember new words.

CHAPTER 1: CORE VOCABULARY – PART I

1. AMBIVALENT – mixed feelings
2. ANOMALY and ATYPICAL – a deviation from the norm
3. SARCASTIC, SARDONIC, SNIDE – derisive mocking comments
4. DEARTH and PAUCITY – a scarcity or shortage
5. PRATTLE – to babble incessantly
6. WRY and DROLL – dry humor
7. UNCONVENTIONAL and UNORTHODOX – not ordinary or typical
8. PAINSTAKING, METICULOUS, EXACTING – highly detailed
9. AUDACIOUS – very bold; daring
10. INDIFFERENT and APATHETIC – lack of interest or concern
11. DIFFIDENT – lacking self-confidence
12. PRAGMATIC – practical, sensible
13. EVOCATION – an imaginative recreation
14. PRESUMPTUOUS – overbearing; impertinently bold
15. RECALCITRANT and OBDURATE – very stubborn, defiant
16. BOON – a timely benefit
    BANE – a source of harm
17. CLANDESTINE and SURREPTITIOUS – secretive; not aboveboard; covert
18. AFFABLE, AMIABLE, GENIAL, GREGARIOUS – agreeable; friendly

19. AUSTERE – bare, NOT ornate

    AUSTERITY – enforced economy

20. ALTRUISTIC – unselfish concern for others

21. AMBIGUOUS – unclear; not definitive

22. UPBRAID, REPROACH, CASTIGATE,

    – to scold; rebuke

23. NOSTALGIA – a sentimental longing for the past

24. CONJECTURE and SUPPOSITION – an inference

25. OBSOLETE, ARCHAIC, ANTIQUATED

    – no longer in use

26. AUSPICIOUS and PROPITIOUS – very favorable

27. MOROSE and DESPONDENT – very depressed

28. IMPASSE – failure to reach an agreement

29. ANACHRONISM – not in the proper time period

30. BELIE – to give a false impression

31. MITIGATE, MOLLIFY, ASSUAGE, ALLEVIATE

    – to ease; relieve; lessen

32. COVET – to strongly desire; to crave

33. ANTITHESIS, ANTITHETICAL, ANTIPODAL

    – direct opposite

34. PROTOTYPE – an original model

35. ALOOF – detached; reserved

36. TRITE, HACKNEYED, PEDESTRIAN, PLATITUDINOUS, BANAL, INSIPID

    – commonplace

37. ANTECEDENT, FORERUNNER, PRECURSOR

    – a preceding event

38. PLAUSIBLE - believable

IMPLAUSIBLE – not believable

39. PRUDENT – careful; cautious

40. AESTHETIC – an appreciation of what is beautiful or attractive

41. PARADOX – a seeming contradiction that expresses a truth

42. ENIGMATIC and INSCRUTABLE – mysterious; baffling

43. ACQUIESCE – to comply

44. NAÏVE, GULLIBLE, CREDULOUS – unsophisticated

45. AUTONOMOUS - independent

46. FUTILE – doomed to failure

47. INDIGENOUS and ENDEMIC – native to an area

48. UBIQUITOUS and PREVALENT – everywhere; widespread; prevalent

49. PANDEMIC – widespread epidemic

50. FORTITUDE – strength of mind

CHAPTER 2: CORE VOCABULARY – PART II

51. DIMINUTIVE – very small
52. TRIVIAL and MINUTIAE – minor, everyday details
53. EXHORT – to strongly encourage
54. ANTIPATHY,ANIMOSITY, RANCOR – strong dislike
55. DIGRESS – to depart from a subject
56. TENACIOUS – showing great determination
57. INDULGENT – overly tolerant
58. POLARIZE and DIVISIVE – to break into opposing factions
59. NEBULOUS – vague; lacking a fully developed form
60. ANALOGY and ANALOGOUS – a similarity or likeness
61. FLEETING and EPHEMERAL – very brief; short lived
62. PENCHANT and PREDILECTION – a preference for something; an inclination
63. CAPRICIOUS and MERCURIAL – fickle; constantly shifting moods
64. BOORISH, UNCOUTH, CRASS – vulgar; crude
65. INDIGNANT – outrage at something that is unjust
66. INNUENDO – a veiled reference
67. THWART and STYMIE – to stop; frustrate
68. ADROIT, DEFT, ADEPT, DEXTEROUS - skillful
69. ADMONISH – to earnestly caution

70. INCONTROVERTIBLE – indisputable; beyond doubt

71. VORACIOUS and RAVENOUS – a huge appetite; cannot be satisfied; insatiable

72. CALLOUS - insensitive

73. INTREPID and UNDAUNTED – fearless; courageous

74. NONCHALANT – casual indifference

75. CONVOLUTED – twisted; intricate

76. ITINERANT – mobile; not sedentary

itinerary: trips (move around on trips)

77. POIGNANT – touching; heartrending

78. IMPETUS – a stimulus or encouragement

79. BUCOLIC, RUSTIC, PASTORAL – charmingly rural

80. EQUANIMITY and UNFLAPPABLE – calmness; composure

81. PANACHE, VERVE, FLAMBOYANT – great vigor and energy, dash

82. PROVOCATIVE – provokes controversy

83. PLACID and SERENE – very calm; quiet

84. FORTUITOUS – an accidental but fortunate occurrence *fortunate*

85. DISPEL – to drive away; scatter

86. AMALGAM – a mixture; combination of different elements

87. VIABLE and FEASIBLE - possible

88. ANGUISH – agonizing physical or mental pain

89. INTEMPERATE – lacking restraint; excessive
TEMPERATE – exercising moderation

90. SUPERFICIAL – shallow; lacking depth

91. LAUD, EXTOL, TOUT, ACCLAIM – praise; applaud

92. DISMISSIVE – to reject; disregard

93. DISPARAGE – belittle; slight

94. POMPOUS – pretentious; filled with excessive self-importance

95. CRYPTIC – mysterious; having a hidden meaning

96. SUBTLE – a gradual almost imperceptible change

97. DISPARITY – an inequality; an imbalance

98. CURTAIL – to cut short or reduce

99. INNOCUOUS - harmless

100. DIATRIBE and TIRADE – a bitter denunciation

CHAPTER 3: YOU MEET THE MOST INTERESTING PEOPLE ON THE SAT

101. CHARLATAN – a fake; a fraud; a cheat
102. SKEPTIC – a doubter
103. RHETORICIAN – an eloquent writer or speaker
104. HEDONIST – seeker of pleasure
105. ASCETIC – a person who leads a life of self-denial
106. RACONTEUR – a person who excels in telling anecdotes
107. ICONOCLAST – someone who attacks cherished ideas and institutions
108. DILETTANTE – an amateur or dabbler
109. PARTISAN – a person with biased beliefs *support one PARTY*
110. MENTOR – a teacher; a guide; an advisor
   ACOLYTE – a devoted student
111. DEMAGOGUE – a speaker who appeals to emotions, fears or prejudices
112. AUTOMATON – a person who acts in a mechanical fashion; a mindless follower
113. RECLUSE – a person who leads a secluded, solitary life
114. BUNGLER – a clumsy or inept person
115. CLAIRVOYANT – a person who uses intuition to see into the future; a seer
116. PROGNOSTICATOR – a person who makes predictions based upon data
117. PUNDIT – a professional commentator
118. ZEALOT – a very enthusiastic person

119. NEOPHYTE, NOVICE and GREENHORN – a beginner

120. BENEFACTOR – a person who gives gifts
     BENEFICIARY – a person who receives benefits

121. DISSEMBLER and PREVARICATOR – a liar; deceiver

122. PROPONENT and ADVOCATE – a champion of a cause

123. PRODIGY – a young genius

124. ORACLE – a person who is a source of wise counsel and prophetic advice

125. MISANTHROPE – a person who hates humankind

126. INNOVATOR – a person who introduces something new

127. SYCOPHANT and OBSEQUIOUS – a person who behaves in a servile manner; a toady

128. STOIC – a person who is impassive and emotionless

129. REPROBATE – a morally unprincipled person

130. RENEGADE – a disloyal person

CHAPTER 4: EVERY SAT WORD HAS A HISTORY

131. DRACONIAN – very strict laws and rules

132. LACONIC, SUCCINCT, TERSE – very concise; brief

133. SPARTAN – plain; simple

134. HALCYON – idyllically calm and tranquil

135. SOPHISTRY – a deliberately misleading argument

136. CHIMERICAL – a fantastic scheme; unchecked imagination

137. OSTRACIZE – to deliberately exclude from a group

138. IMPECUNIOUS – poor; penniless; not affluent

139. NEFARIOUS – extremely wicked; vile

140. JOVIAL and JOCULAR – good-humored; cheerful

141. DIRGE – a funeral hymn; mournful music

142. MAUDLIN – excessively sentimental

143. QUIXOTIC – foolishly impractical

144. PANDEMONIUM – a wild uproar; tumult

145. MARTINET – a strict disciplinarian

146. FIASCO and DEBACLE – a complete failure

147. BOWDLERIZE – to remove or delete objectionable parts of a book

148. GALVANIZE – to electrify; stir into action

149. PICAYUNE – something of small value; petty; trifling

150. GERRYMANDER – to divide a district so as to give one side an advantage

151. MAVERICK – an independent person
152. JUGGERNAUT – an irresistible force
153. SERENDIPITY – an accidental but fortunate discovery
154. ZENITH and APEX – the highest point
155. NADIR – the lowest point

CHAPTER 5: THE MIGHTY PREFIXES

156. EXPUNGE, EXCISE, EXPURGATE – delete; remove

157. ECCENTRIC – an odd, unconventional person

158. EXTRICATE – to get out of a difficult situation

159. EXEMPLARY - outstanding

160. ENUMERATE – to list; to tick off

161. ELUSIVE – out of reach; difficult to catch

162. EXORBITANT – unreasonably expensive

163. REPUDIATE, RECANT, RENOUNCE – to take back; disavow

164. REDUNDANT – doing or saying something again and again

165. RELINQUISH – to give something back

166. RESILIENT – to bounce back

167. REAFFIRM – to assert again

168. RETICENT – to hold back one's thoughts and feelings

169. REBUFF – to repel or drive back; to reject

170. RENOVATE – to make new again

171. REJUVENATE – to make young again

172. RESURGENT – to rise again; surge back

173. DELETERIOUS – harmful; injurious

174. DECRY – to express strong disapproval

175. DESPONDENT and FORLORN – feeling downcast; dejected

176. DENOUNCE – to speak against

177. DEMISE – the final ending of something; the downfall

178. DEBUNK – to put down by exposing false claims
179. DERIDE – to put down with contemptuous jeering
180. DEVOID – completely lacking in something
181. IMPECCABLE – faultless; perfect
182. IMPLACABLE – not capable of being appeased
183. INEXORABLE – relentless, unstoppable
184. INCOHERENT – lacking organization or logic
185. INSURMOUNTABLE – not capable of being overcome
186. IRREVERENT – lacking proper respect; disrespectful
187. CIRCUMSPECT and PRUDENT – cautious; careful
188. CIRCUITOUS – circular and therefore indirect
189. CIRCUMVENT – to avoid by artful maneuvering
190. CIRCUMSCRIBE – to narrowly restrict; to limit action; to draw a line around
191. MAGNANIMOUS – generous and forgiving
192. ERRONEOUS – filled with errors; wrong
193. MOMENTOUS – of great importance
194. MELLIFLUOUS – smooth and sweet flowing
195. OMINOUS – threatening and menacing
196. ACRIMONIOUS – great bitterness
197. COPIOUS – abundant; a great amount
198. ABSTEMIOUS – moderate in eating and drinking
199. MALODOROUS – foul smelling
200. TEDIOUS – boring and tiresome

Index

INDEX

INDEX

INDEX

WORD ....**Main Page**, Other Page(s)

mode offsegment

.x

Provocative **48**, 49
Prudent **21**, 130
Pundit 56, **73**, 129
Quixotic **98**, 99

Raconteur **68**
Rancor **35**, 134
Ravenous **43**, 44
Reaffirm **120**
Rebuff **121**
Recalcitrant **9**, 121
Recant **118**
Recluse **71**
Redundant **118**, 119
Rejuvenate **122**
Relinquish **119**
Renegade **80**
Renounce **118**
Renovate **121**
Reproach **12**
Reprobate **79**
Repudiate **118**
Resilient **119**, 120, 122
Resolute 15
Resurgent **122**
Reticent **120**
Rhetorician **67**
Rustic **47**

Sabotage 35
Saga 54, 70
Sarcastic **3**, 19, 44
Sardonic 3
Sedentary **45**
Seer **72**
Seminal **78**
Serendipity **105**, 106
Serene **49**
Skeptic 43, **66**, 67, 72, 73, 128

INDEX

Breinigsville, PA USA
23 March 2011
258262BV00002B/86/P